ACKNOWLEDGEMENTS

THANK YOU GOD
For the inspiration

KEN SOBEL
Special thanks for your support

MARCIA MORAN
For sharing her insight on cold reading workshops

RAOUL RIZIK
For introducing me to the cold reading concept

TENE CARTER
MORRIS NASH
For your contributions as interns

HELEN HARPER
She knows why

FAMILY & FRIENDS
For all their help and support

Heaven Sent Publishing 6th Edition
Angel Harper -Author/Publisher (323) 467-7782

Published by Heaven Sent Publishing
www.coldreading.com

Edited by Shirley Jordan
Layout by JESIMS.com

ISBN#: 0-9630551-4-3

Library of Congress Control Number: 2004104724
North Charleston, South Carolina

All rights are reserved. No part of this publication may be reproduced or transmitted in any form or by any means, electronic or mechanical, including photocopying and recording, or by any information storage or retrieval system, without prior written permission from the publisher or author.

INTRODUCTION

FROM THE PUBLISHER

It's the 21st century and I want to encourage you to embrace it by taking charge of your career. Don't depend on your agent or manager to get your career going. Don't continue to do the same things you did last year and expect improvement. The studio system of yesterday, that of making actors into stars, doesn't exist anymore. Instead, to help build and shape their careers, actors are attending cold reading workshops. This system benefits both the newcomers to the business as well as the advanced actor. Cold reading workshops have been under much controversy and scrutiny in the past few years. I have added some new information to address those issues so that you may determine the value of these workshops for yourself. Go ahead. Have the career you dreamed of. Stop talking about what you will do and instead do it. Hollywood 2004 and beyond demands an aggressive and knowledgeable approach to your acting career. Did you make any new decisions? Are you determined to make them happen? Are you enthusiastic or jaded about your career?

This is the 6th edition of my book and it is still a labor of love, dedicated to the industry that I love – ACTING. Thank you for your helpful suggestions as to how to make this book as effective as possible. I've included some of them in this edition. I'm grateful for your continued support.

DEDICATION

THIS BOOK IS DEDICATED TO:

- Actors who want to take charge of their own careers.
- Actors who want to learn how to do a "winning" cold reading.
- Actors who have a serious desire to maintain accurate and organized information about the cold reading workshops they have attended.
- Actors who would like to get the most for their money when attending workshops.

Read on. You may find the keys to your success!

MASTER THE ART OF COLD READING

CONTENTS

Introduction (From the Publisher) iv
From the Editor 2
Letter to the Publisher 3

Chapter One 5
About Cold Reading Workshops 5
Workshop Procedures 7
How to Select a Cold Reading Workshop 8
Casting Director, Casting Assistant,
  Casting Associate ... Who Does What? 8
Pros and Cons 9

Chapter Two 13
Technique Helps! 13
Technique Class Listing 14

Chapter Three 17
Workshop Profiles 17
Workshop Listings 31
New CD Workshop Guidelines/
  Industry Commentaries 33
Free Alternatives 37

Chapter Four 39
Tips From Industry Professionals 39
Casting Directors 39
Agents & Managers 47
Teachers & Coaches 48
Directors 52
Producers 54
Actorspeak 57
Academia 63

Chapter Five 67
Cold Reading For the Young Actor 67

Chapter Six 75
Cold Reading For Voice-Overs 75
Classes for Voice-Overs 85

CONTENTS

Chapter Seven 87
Chicken Soup for Your Career 87

Chapter Eight 113
Rounding Out Your Career...with other helpful
   industry services! 113

Chapter Nine 121
If You're Online...   121

Appendices 123
Sample Questions to Ask in a Cold Reading Workshop 123
Sample Follow-Up Post Card 124
Sample Workshop Information Forms 125
About the Author 127
About the Editor 128
Be A Volunteer 129
"Special Order" and Other Book Locales 130
A Very Special Thanks 132

FROM THE EDITOR

While editing this 6th edition of Master the Art of Cold Reading, many interesting things caught my eye. For starters, cold reading workshops have definitely grown in number and strength by leaps and bounds! We are all realizing now that, yes, being in the right place at the right time with the right goods, can be lucrative. With the expansion of cable, independent producers, movies straight-to-video as well as those cast here but shot outside of the country, the need to connect and share information is greater than ever. And where better than a cold reading workshop!

Other aspects of our industry that have reinvented themselves are classes. We now have classes to aid us in spiritually, emotionally, and physically finding those deep inner sanctums which enhance our personal qualities on the way to sculpting the actors we strive to be. We can then apply this information to our scene study and cold reading classes, which will aid in developing a more expedient route in bringing truth and depth to our work as actors.

Technology has also made it possible for an actor to be seen and heard without moving much more than one's point and click finger. With the influx of the many on-line casting facilities and promotional tools available, communication from all sides of the table has been made easier, more efficient, and certainly more interesting.

But, as much as things change, some things still remain the same. No matter where the many testimonies and bits of advice in this book have come from over the years, this advice remains true; cold reading workshops are a wonderful supplement to everything else you do to promote your career. You must understand that they do not, however, take the place of acting classes. A workshop relies on the quality of its performers and the strength of their industry guests to sustain success and longevity. Give them the respect they deserve and, in turn, they will serve you well. But don't take my word for it. These pages contain many words of wisdom from people who have "been there, done that". We also have new input from industry professionals who have graciously offered advice on just about every aspect necessary to help transform you into a more marketable, well-informed, focused, working actor. Enjoy!

LETTER TO THE PUBLISHER

Dear Angel,

I'm delighted to share my thoughts and experiences regarding cold reading. I started going to cold reading workshops as soon as I found out about them. I regularly attended workshops at In The Act, Reel Pros, Seenworks and One on One. During the first year I went to three a week. I was lucky I could afford this. I only saw the main casting directors and kept a record of who they were, where they were from, addressed, special likes and dislikes. I took the calendars to my agents and asked them to check off who they wanted me to see. I was surprised at how many they rejected because they weren't working or were, for me, not worth seeing at the time. I also found that all the workshops have pretty much the same people, so if I miss someone at one, I can pick them up in another. I often hear older actors complain that they shouldn't have to pay for meeting an industry professional. BULL! I am my own business. No business succeeds without advertising and development. And a casting director is a potential buyer for my business. Every actor should regularly budget for promoting his or her business.

I think the biggest mistake young actors make is in pacing. They are so eager to show how emotionally deep they can get that they slow down the reading. The sides also have a pivotal point in them, which they miss, because they haven't analyzed them properly. Some other observations I've seen actors do that harm their overall presentation are as follows:

1. Tucking one's hair behind one's ear is not a substitute for emotion. If your hair falls in your face, do something with it before you begin. If you do this unconsciously, get someone to count how many times you do it in a scene. Ditto with slapping your leg to emphasize a point.

2. Most of the casting directors you see are those who cast sit-coms. It ain't Shakespeare. It's got a beat and a pace. Figure out where the gag lines are and play the words, not the comedy. It is usually written to be funny, and funny is usually best when played straight.

3. Young girls should try to dress appropriately and not wear skirts too short (especially when doing a scene seated) or anything too outlandish. It takes away from your performance.

Conversely, the following are some things you should do to help yourself at cold readings:

1. Learn how not to upstage yourself or your partner and get quickly to your next line.

2. Be on time. If a workshop starts at 7:30, be seated by at least 7:20.

3. If you give a guest a tape, include a large, self-addressed, stamped manila envelope with it. You'll get them back more often.

Good Luck!
Kathy Joosten

Kathy Joosten was also on hand during the controversial proceedings concerning cold reading workshops and was instrumental in helping form the guidelines we now have. For more on the guidelines, see page 44, New CD Workshop Guidelines.

CHAPTER ONE

ABOUT COLD READING WORKSHOPS...

A cold reading is just that - a cold reading. You do not come with prepared scripts. The workshop guest or coordinator will provide all materials. However, it is possible to have prepared three to five minute scenes for specific workshops. Cold readings are difficult, and actors, as well as industry guests, want the best representation of your talent.

Arrive at least fifteen minutes early. Workshops start promptly. An early arrival gives you an opportunity to sign in, mingle with the other actors and relax. Establish a good rapport with your fellow actors. You normally do not know in advance with whom you may be paired to read a scene. You increase the chances for a strong and confident reading if you are comfortable with your partner. Therefore, be friendly and professional with all the actors you meet.

The workshop guest may open the session with a question and answer period. This is your opportunity to get to know the guest personally. This is also another good reason for being on time. There also may be occasions when the question and answer period comes after all readings have been completed and critiqued. Use the worksheets and guides included in this journal as your permanent records for documenting important details about the session.

The workshop guest will then pair you up with an acting partner and hand out scripts. Since this is not an actual casting session, the sides may not be exactly the right roles you usually audition for, however, the industry guest is aware of this and certainly won't hold it against you. Your job is to make the scene believable, which will demonstrate the power of your acting.

You and your partner will have approximately twenty minutes to review the script. When you get your sides, go over them immediately and be open to suggestions from your partner as to the best approach to the scene. Remember that you both want to perform a memorable scene. A workshop coordinator will announce when it is time to start performing the scenes. Once everyone is settled, the

MASTER THE ART OF COLD READING

workshop guest will either choose the order of scene appearances or ask for volunteers. Workshops last between two and three hours, depending on the number of actors attending and the length of scenes read. The average scene will last from three to five minutes.

Although you have sent your headshot and resume in with your payment for the workshop, never leave home without it! Anything can happen, so, like a real audition, always be prepared. If you have several different headshots, decide on the one that would best sell you for this specific workshop guest. You don't get extra points for being confused about how to sell yourself, so don't ask the workshop guest to decide for you. If it's a sitcom workshop, you may want to give your commercial photo or that easy-going photo you never use. Naturally, for the "soap" workshops, you want to give your best glamour shot. Most of all be honest with yourself. If you are a character actor, don't give a glamour photo that won't look like you that night, or in the near future. Typecasting is not a bad word, especially when you're new in town. Casting directors need to know how to cast you and that they can count on your delivery being consistent. You will be allowed to branch out and express your many character styles as you become more established.

A word to the wise. Keep your resume simple and truthful. When you present yourself realistically (headshot) and honestly (resume), you make the best impression. Some industry guests will question your resume credentials. There's nothing worse than being caught in a lie. O.K., you have the right picture and at the very least, a believable resume. Now, what should you wear? Remember - it's your first impression. Casual, neat and clean will work fine. However, if you have a particular way you want to be typecast, then wear you best "kooky" comedic outfit or strong professional attire. Whatever you decide, be comfortable or you won't work well.

Workshop guests conduct their workshops in different ways. There is the silent type who remains poker-faced and offers no reaction to a performance. Others make brief comments at the end of a scene: "Very nice." "The pacing was off." "Very believable." My favorite is the guest that "directs" the actor during the scene. This type of director may stop the reading and suggest a different approach. This gives the actor an additional opportunity to demonstrate versatility as well as the ability to take direction.

Most guests make mental notes on your performance and write comments on your photo. Some guests have very sophisticated filing systems to help them remember the workshop actors they meet. There are still no guarantees, but you do have the satisfaction of knowing that your picture is on file and not thrown out.

As a courtesy to your fellow actors, you should stay until the workshop has ended. Believe me, you can learn a great deal from watching the other performances. If you have personal reasons for leaving early, let the workshop coordinator know in advance. The coordinator will make the workshop guest aware and you will not appear inconsiderate.

It is also considerate to be very brief in saying goodbye to the guest at the end of the workshop. You will make no significant "brownie points" by trying to monopolize guests when they are leaving. A sincere smile, handshake and thank you is both professional and sufficient. A follow-up post card will allow you to personalize your meeting and is an excellent excuse to remind the guest of who you are. (See samples at the end of the book.)

Don't forget! It is also a good idea to have on hand a reel of your work. Not all guests will take one, but it doesn't hurt to ask. After all it's yet another chance to promote your abilities. Make sure to include a SASE for quicker return and as a courtesy to the guest.

Workshop Procedures
Workshop reservations are taken on a first-come, first-served basis. Some workshops require SAG, AFTRA or AEA membership. Auditions may be required at some workshops, unless a current member is referring you. Others may treat the first class as your audition.

Payment/Cancellations
In addition to cash and checks, some workshops accept credit cards. Workshops must be paid for in advance. Some workshops may place reservations received without payment on standby status (until payment is received). Remember, only the confirmed reservation is a paid reservation.

Workshops may require from 48 hours to as much as a 72 hour notice of your cancellation, in order that you receive a refund or credit for your deposit. Multiple session workshops may require that you cancel up to two weeks prior to the beginning of the first session. Latecomers run the risk of forfeiting their space and session fee. Most workshops require your presence no later than ten minutes after the scheduled starting time. A few allow you fifteen minutes. Come in later and you're probably out.

In addition to an actor's need to cancel, workshop guests scheduled to conduct the workshops may change. Therefore, be prepared for such changes. Fortunately, it doesn't happen often enough for it to be a major problem. When there are changes, you are notified and given an opportunity to reschedule for that workshop. If a workshop guest cancels on a particular day, a last minute guest may be substituted. Sometimes the replacement is more appropriate for you than the person who was originally scheduled. So, don't be too disappointed as you may get a better opportunity.

How to Select a Cold Reading Workshop
While convenience is a prime factor for most actors, finding a cold reading workshop group that you feel compatible with is more important. I strongly recommend, if possible, that you audit a cold reading workshop first. You will get a feel for the level of talent in the workshop. You will also be able to observe how organized and friendly the workshop is. Feeling relaxed with a group you have joined gives you a real boost and a sense of support when you read.

It may be to your advantage to get on the list of all available cold reading workshops, then base your workshop selection(s) on the guests who are scheduled. Remember, the goal is to meet people who are casting shows that you have the best chance to work on, based upon your "look" and acting style. For example, you have a great look for soaps. You should to read for a casting director from a soap opera. The appropriate casting director for that type of show may not be scheduled to appear at the workshop you regularly attend. In this case, you may need to attend a workshop that will afford you an opportunity to read for such a casting director.

Casting Director, Casting Assistant, Casting Associate...Who Does What?
It is very important that actors understand the responsibilities and

power of the casting associate and casting assistant. In order to understand the position of the casting associate and assistant, a review of the director's job is in order. It is important to note that the Casting Society of America (CSA) has no official definition of the casting director's duties. Remember, too, that there is no requirement that a casting director be a member of the CSA.

A casting director is hired by the producer or network to read a script and find actors that will compliment the characters in that script. A casting director may receive a minimum of 500 headshots and resumes submitted for each role. That role may be for a character with as little as one line. Casting directors cast the leading, supporting and featured roles of a script. There are also many casting services, dedicated exclusively to casting "extras" (non-speaking roles).

To help sort through this competitive process, casting directors hire associates and assistants, based on the size of the casting project. Casting associates work very closely with the casting director. The casting associate will pre-read actors for the casting director and often read with an actor during producer callbacks. Many casting directors become casting associates when they are not working on a project of their own. It's important to keep in mind that titles don't always reveal the extent of the responsibility or power of a casting associate or assistant.

Generally, casting assistants have more secretarial duties. Don't take this for granted, though. These are the people that sort through the hundreds of headshots and organize auditions for the casting directors.

If you attend a workshop that has a casting associate or assistant as a guest, instead of a casting director, ask how their offices divides the casting responsibility. Remember, you can always learn something from someone who has an inside track to the industry.

The Pros & Cons of Cold Readings
Long before I arrived in Los Angeles, I was warned that agents don't do anything for their clients. I was constantly told that you have to submit yourself for roles, bug your agent and change agents frequently. One avenue for breaking into the business that I was not

aware of until I arrived in Los Angeles is by participating in cold reading workshops.

It is important to be realistic about opportunities to read for a role; whether it is for an audition or a paid workshop. It is very rare that actors get a job the first time they read for a casting director. However, a memorable impression will almost guarantee you another opportunity, perhaps for another role was that was meant for you and you alone.

The first step to being a working actor in Los Angeles is to audition often. One way of interpreting auditions is to approach them as an opportunity for industry professionals to see your acting skills. Cold reading workshops allow you to do that on a regular basis.

If you really want to take charge of your career, you do not have to wait for your agent or manager to arrange an appointment with a casting director. Just sign up for cold reading workshops.

There are both positive and negative attitudes toward cold reading workshops.

First, the negative:
Some of the industry population views the concept of cold reading workshops as a paid audition. They feel that they are a rip-off because actors pay for the privilege of reading for casting directors. There is a clear disclaimer on most reputable cold reading workshop brochures that says; "The presence of a casting director is not a guarantee of employment." Well, I say getting a free audition is no guarantee of work either. You should be aware that some people in the industry find these workshops legal, but unethical.

Onto the positive side:
Cold reading workshops provide an avenue for talented actors to showcase their abilities to producers, agents, directors and casting directors. They are also a very viable means to acquiring insight into how this business works. Actors normally must wait for an audition or a "general appointment" (general) to meet a casting director. However, these days casting directors don't have the time to do generals. Generals are more of a "getting to know you" session. Don't depend on a general appointment as an opportunity to

showcase your talent. Think of it as a fact-finding trip for all parties. An agent or manager must be have a lot of clout to get a general for you. If you have a very persuasive agent or manager, you probably will not need cold reading workshops. However, if you are talented and believe all you need is an opportunity to be seen, cold reading workshop may be one answer.

Which brings us back to why cold reading workshops have become so popular, especially with new talent. It is one way that you can take charge of your career. You, the actor, decide which casting directors are casting productions that you think are right for you. You can sign up to work before that casting director and give a performance to remember. While there are still no guarantees, if you are talented, you will be remembered. The next time your photograph comes across that casting director's desk, he or she will be familiar, not only with your face, but with your work. It could make the difference between your photograph being tossed aside or held aside.

There are no shortcuts to success. Actors find success in their own, unique way. However, if you have the right business skills and are well organized, you can separate yourself from the pack. This journal gives you a way of keeping track of cold reading workshops that you attend, the workshop guests you meet and the proper way to follow up and make a good impression at a subsequent audition.

MASTER THE ART OF COLD READING

CHAPTER TWO

TECHNIQUE HELPS!

This section supplies you with a list of acting coaches, schools and people that specialize in teaching cold reading techniques. The following is just a sampling of professionals available to help you in the Los Angeles area. Since everyone will claim to be the best, it is important for you to interview the instructor and audit a class when possible. Do this before you invest your money. Ask your agent or other actors for their opinion.

Assess your needs as an actor. If you don't have strong acting skills, good cold reading techniques may get you a job, but they won't sustain you on the job. Don't waste your money taking cold reading classes if you don't have strong acting skills.

Don't be fooled or persuaded to sign up with someone who promises you industry contacts. Once you work with the right cold reading instructor for your level, you will find yourself landing more auditions, producer callbacks and JOBS!

This is a very subtle issue that is not usually talked about. There are various levels of acting skills that may be grouped in a workshop. This means some places take anybody from anywhere and some are more discerning. You want to be in a workshop where the talent is consistently good and the actors are getting called in. Do your research. Find out if the actors are auditioned beforehand. Again, ask other actors and industry people you meet about workshops they might frequent.

MASTER THE ART OF COLD READING

COLD READING TECHNIQUE CLASSES (partial listing)

Joel Asher 818-785-1551
www.joel-asher-studio.com

Robert Burgos *(coaches privately)* 323-653-5947

Ron Burris   Ronburris@earthlink.net 323-953-2823
www.Ronburris.com
June Chandler 626-355-4572

Vincent Chase 323-851-9942

Kim Darby 818-985-0666
www.kimdarby.com

Piero Dusa Acting Conservatory 310-656-8070
www.Pierodusa.com

Steve Eastin 818-980-9828

Allen Fawcett www.Killerreel.com 818-763-7399

Alan Feinstein/Paul Tuerpe 323-650-7766
www.Feinstein-Tuerpe.com

Ellen Gerstein 323-852-0276

Bruce Glover *(Inner Technique)* 310-398-2539

Maria Gobetti 818-843-9253

Margie Haber 323-969-8089

Lena Harris 310-226-7034

Kimberly Jentzen 818-779-7770

Anita Jesse 323-876-2870

CHAPTER 2

David Kagen 818-752-9678
www.davidkagen.com

David Lehman 818-845-1549

Sy Richardson 661-252-6169

Joe Salazar 323-882-6433

Melissa Skoff 323-468-4556

Millie Slavin 310-582-3485

Teri Tunder 323-969-0795

Wallace Audition Technique 323-960-7852

Doug Warhit 310-479-5647

Caryn West 323-876-0394

MASTER THE ART OF COLD READING

TTechnique Class Listing

CHAPTER THREE
WORKSHOP PROFILES

AIA - Action In Acting

I began my casting career with CBS Television. I enjoyed casting so much that I went into full-service casting independently. I opened Katy & Co., a full service casting company. I have cast over 100 feature films, TV shows and commercials. My clients include Zucker Brothers Productions, Fox-TV, Lynch Entertainment, McDonalds, Reebok, Sizzler, and more. In addition, I have cast music videos for such artists as Phil Collins, Michael Bolton and Genesis.

From my experience as a casting director, I recognized the need for actors to continually showcase themselves and network with industry professionals - most importantly those who have the ability to hire them. That is when I opened Action in Acting, one of L.A.'s top full-service networking companies for actors. I wanted to create an environment where actors could network themselves in a professional, supportive and friendly environment. Action In Acting provides the actors with the opportunity not only to showcase their talents to top directors, producers, casting directors and agents, but also to train with some of the most talented coaches in L.A. in the areas of scene study, cold reading, soap, commercial and improv.

Due to the high caliber of actors, we are very lucky to have such distinguished guests who come to Action In Acting exclusively. Every workshop is professionally produced and we offer each actor the opportunity for a one-on-one interview with guests prior to the beginning of the workshop. Due to the nurturing atmosphere of Action in Acting, actors enjoy the constant support that is provided for them each evening.

Action In Acting has so many success stories to share. Since we opened in 1990, over 1,000 of our actors have worked on films, TV shows, soaps, commercials and music videos. Every day, actors call with news of their most recent success stories.

Act Now!
Kenna Dean

Act Now! is a networking company that was established 6 years ago with the intention of helping actors further their careers by meeting, learning from and performing for industry professionals including casting directors, producers, directors and agents. Act Now! was founded by Kenna Dean, a twenty three year veteran of the entertainment business. Our discriminating staff provides ongoing guidance and support to help each actor set and meet his and her professional goals. At Act Now!, we understand the importance of treating the business of acting as a business. Therefore we require a thorough interview and reading of all of the actors that come through the doors. This insures the highest quality of talent and professionalism in our workshops. What sets Act Now! apart from all of our competitors is our collection of talented actors, as well as our professional environment, personal attention and commitment to excellence.

Call Act Now!: (818) 840-2795 or visit their website at www.actnownetwork.com

The Actors Edge
Christina Ferra

The Actors Edge workshop was established in 1990 with the intention of training a small number of dedicated actors who have that special something extra that will enable them to succeed. As time progressed, this small institution began to grow and grow, making us one of the most respected schools in the Los Angeles area. Unlike most schools, we never allow our class size to grow above fourteen students. This gives you the opportunity to perform at every class meeting for a substantial amount of time. The Actors Edge is more than just a quality workshop. It's a supportive environment for the actor who is serious about getting ahead. It's a positive place to come and meet once a week to keep working out and growing as an actor.

Christina Ferra, president of The Actors Edge, teaches all of the intermediate and master classes. She has studied with the best acting teachers from around the world and shares these skills with her students. Christina casts principle roles for television and film. Her expert eye helps the actor to see himself as the casting director sees him when he goes out for those very important acting roles. Unlike most casting directors who run a workshop or showcase group, she also understands and teaches the acting techniques that she used successfully during her early years as a professional working actor. Her techniques won her the starring role in a Broadway play, national commercials, and even cartoon voice-overs for feature films. She holds a two month comprehensive cold reading workshop each year. Once you are a member, you are eligible to perform in the agency showcase as well as our Actors Edge television show.

The Actors Edge is dedicated to promoting you and your career. We take pride in our work, and take it very seriously. We ask that you do the same and give a 100% commitment when you become a member. We specialize in cold reading and audition technique.

The Actorsite
JP Turnbull
The Actorsite is a community of actors and our members have found much success by doing the 9 basic steps to career success, and workshops is just one of the steps.

We have two locations:
5654 Cahuenga
North Hollywood, CA 91601
818.787.6344

7033 Sunset #205
Los Angeles, CA 90028
323.957.1159

For more information, please visit our website:
http://www.actorsite.com

The Casting Break
Robin Lee Knoll
Our Start: We've been in business for 8 1/2 years. Our company was started by a group of professional actors who wanted to create a positive, supportive atmosphere for professional actors and industry professionals to meet and learn from each other. Our staff is made up of actors and producers.

Our Actors: We're known for having a many working actors. We love the fact that practically any night we turn on the TV, we see at least

MASTER THE ART OF COLD READING

one of our actors in a guest-starring role on a sit-com or episodic or on a commercial. We don't advertise in the trades because we do not want to attract beginner actors; all of our actors are referred by agents, producers, etc., word-of-mouth, theatre companies, and so on. This has helped us to keep a high level of talent.

The Casting Break is an intimate showcase/workshop that takes pride in its comfortable, supportive and non-competitive atmosphere. We are encouraged by the fact that many of our industry guests tell us that they have never seen so many good actors in one night. We love it when our actors give us feedback on what they like AND suggestions for serving them better.

Aside from numerous cold reading (with some prepared scenes or monologues as is the guest's preference) workshops with well established industry professionals, we also offer specialty workshops, such as:

"How To Promote Yourself As An Actor" by one of LA's top publicists, *"Colors On-Camera"* with Jill Kirsh, owner of The Color Company, *"Michael Donovan's On-Camera Commercial Intensive"* – exclusively at Casting Break, and *"How To Write Your Own Performance Material"* with Michael Hauge, one of the nation's top scriptwriting consultants.

Note:
To Our Casting Break Family,
This is a quick note to keep you in the loop regarding the exciting changes that are going on at The Casting Break. First, we want to thank all of you for being such a wonderful support system to each other, to our staff and to us. Many of you have been coming to The Casting Break since the first day we opened over 8 years ago. We are thrilled that Actorsite is joining forces with us so that we (Actorsite and The Casting Break) can continue serving actors, helping you to achieve your goals in the entertainment industry. Be sure to log on to www.actorsite.com to see the current calendar of events being held at The Casting Break location. More and more terrific guests are being scheduled each week, so keep checking in for updates. Again, we thank you for sharing your talents with us and we thank you for making The Casting Break a safe harbor for so many.
As Always,
Robert and Robin Lee Knoll

Workshop Profiles

CHAPTER 3

The Casting Break: (818) 990-9994
11965 Ventura Blvd. Studio City, CA 91604

The Casting Connection
Bobbi Chandler
The Casting Connection was established in 1985 as one of the original cold reading workshops in Los Angeles. It continues to be one of the longest running, most successful and reputable of the workshops in the area.

I was a professional actress and singer for many years. My credits include film, television, stage and commercials. Prior to moving to Los Angeles, I also worked in broadcasting, advertising, and several other acting-related businesses.

Personally, I like approaching show business as a business! Our workshops are a great combination of acting, marketing and promotion that help increase an actor's chance in the incredibly competitive Los Angeles market. In trying to provide a genuine service to the actors, the casting directors, and other special guests, The Casting Connection's workshops attempt to connect all of their efforts. We are continuing to expand on what the prior owner had already created by incorporating guests with more varied backgrounds, including casting directors, agents, producers and directors.

Most of our actors comment that they like The Casting Connection's workshops because they're structured, but have a comfortable, relaxed and very professional atmosphere. By approaching the workshops from the actors' point of view, we are sensitive to their very best work. The guests seem to enjoy coming here for the same reasons. Therefore, they are able to concentrate on and enjoy the actors' work even more.

We take a personal interest in making the best match for our actors and industry guests by suggesting actors that have the talent and qualities necessary for their current projects. Because of our excellent reputation with these working professionals, these kinds of "casting connections" have resulted in films, theater projects, recurring roles on soaps and episodes and even SAG cards for several of our actors.

MASTER THE ART OF COLD READING

This is part of the extended service we like to provide for the many people that participate in our workshop.

We appreciate suggestions, ideas, needs and try to fulfill specific requests for any guest that our actors would like to meet. We encourage new people to come and audit our workshops and see the high quality of our guests, our actors and our service.

TCN-The Casting Network
Marcia Moran

TCN, established in 1988, has developed a reputation for being LA's Premier Cold Reading Workshop. For years we have been receiving the highest praise and respect from Casting Directors, Agents, Producers and Directors for providing them the opportunity to come together with the Hollywood talent pool and share their expertise with our talented members. We at TCN have long realized that we are the CEOs of our own company and therefore need the following tools: audition techniques, demystifying the audition process, the business of acting, how casting procedures differ between pilots, features, episodics and sitcoms, office etiquette, general trends in casting and the critique of headshots and resumes. We are here to help you learn from the pros how to best market yourself. As a result, we have received hundreds of letters from actors thanking us for providing them a safe environment to help advance in their careers. Our entire friendly and loving staff are all top professional actors and we have always dedicated ourselves to making The Casting Network a win-win for all!

To uphold our high standards of talent, actors are required to pre-audition, at no charge, before being admitted into The Casting Network. You are also allowed one free audit, per person. Once admitted, we offer nightly and weekend workshops plus we offer great discount packs!

If you are interested in joining The Casting Network, check out our website: www.castingnetwork.net. Or call 818-788-4792 and press #3. You can email us at castingnetwork@castingnetwork.net.

Cold reading workshops are a tool to sharpen the actor by continuing to exercise their audition muscle, to better prepare the actor for a

CHAPTER 3

professional and successful career in the industry. We are located at 12500 Riverside Drive, Suite 202, Studio City, CA 91607 Phone: 818-788-4792 Fax: 818-986-3311.

In The Act
Jean St. James

Since its inception fifteen years ago, In The Act has become known as one of the leaders in the cold reading workshop industry. Founder and owner, Jean St. James, had attended a cold reading workshop and was sure that this was an easier way to make connections in the industry than the endless mailers and treks to the studio. At last, an active way to take responsibility for your own career.

In many ways, the industry tries to take advantage of actors. Our goal at ITA is to protect the actors by creating an environment where they can perform with actors that are not only talented but SUPPORTIVE. Our members support each other in endeavors outside the workshops and are thrilled to hear each other's success stories as it elevates our entire platform. It is also our goal to make it affordable, as well as maintaining a high caliber of talent. Actors need to know that if they are going to spend their money, they can be confident that they will get the best. It's about the quality of the work, not about making money.

At ITA, each actor has a real feeling of being responsible for his or her own work, which cuts down the competitive reality which exists in this business. When they come to ITA, they join a supportive and talented nucleus thus enabling them to develop their audition skills, talent, and business connections, so they can leave ITA workshops feeling good about themselves as an actor and better prepared to deal with the real world. Actors who tackle their careers on a day-to-day basis with a feeling of joy and confidence can have an impact on entire business.

CASTING911.com is an on-line spin-off of ITA. It is the only pre-screened on-line talent pool of professional actors. As it is a listing of ITA actors, ITA membership is required. Casting directors can now access actors they've seen at ITA with a click of the button.

In The Act is located at 10015 Venice Blvd (at Clarington) LA, CA

90034. For more information, call (310) 281-7772 or click on www.itaproductions.com

Joel Asher Studio
Joel Asher

Joel Asher's expertise on acting comes from many perspectives. He's been a successful actor, director, writer and teacher. Asher has long been known as one of the country's top acting coaches. His writing credits include his book *"ACTING TECHNIQUE"*, (which has been the text for many acting courses) as well as assignments as a theatre critic for ShowBiz/West and the Winthrop Sun-Transcript, a variety of articles for Drama-Logue and Spotlight Casting.

The Joel Asher Studio presents a 6-week cold reading workshop based on the multiple award-winning video "Getting the Part". This is the best selling video of its kind for actors in the country. The workshop is clear, concise and complete. It offers a format for actors to follow to ensure that they will do their best work in the shortest time. It takes the mystery out of cold reading. The biggest thing that gets in your way is tension. But, if you can develop a few simple techniques that you can use quickly, then you can pick up a script and be interesting, creative and truthful. You can show them, not just the cold reading, but who you are as a person and what you do as an actor. That is what they really want to see.

Included with *"Getting the Part"* in Joel Asher's award-winning video set are CASTING DIRECTORS -*"Tell It Like It Is!"* and AGENTS - *"Tell It Like It Is!"*

Now Casting.Com

NowCasting.com offers cold reading industry workshops as one of its numerous services available to actors. We never advertise workshops as a way to "get hired"; rather we see them as a great educational and marketing/networking tool that helps to demystify the auditioning process and train the actor in the various writing styles and mediums of TV, Film and Commercial projects. As part of the "learning tools" aspect of the workshops, we encourage our actors to bring a VHS tape to record their cold reading scene. By reviewing their scene(s), an actor can reinforce the positive aspects of their cold reading audition

CHAPTER 3

skills and address any negative behavior or habits that may be hindering their ability to "book the job" when at an actual audition.

We're a company run by professional actors and we maintain an actor-friendly environment. Our policies regarding workshops are posted on our site at www.nowcasting.com and we encourage any comments or questions regarding workshops or any of our other services. We require our actors to audition for our cold reading workshops because, as Angel Harper says in this book, "There are many talented and trained actors that do not do well when cold reading." CDs, Associates and Actors all benefit from a more level playing field by our maintaining a talent pool of actors whose cold reading skills are at a professional level.

NowCasting.com (formerly known as LA Actors Online) is run by actors FOR actors and is dedicated to providing the best marketing and networking tools available to the business-minded actor.

Primetime Actors Studio
PrimeTime Actors Studio was formed with the belief that consistent training is one of the most important elements in a successful career. For those at the top, training is a necessary honing of the skills that keep them successful. For those who have not yet achieved their full career potential, training will help them in the intense struggle for success.

PrimeTime Actors Studio offers a comprehensive schedule of classes in film and television techniques for professional, intermediate or beginning actors. Whatever your present qualifications, you can be sure to sharpen your skill through a variety of courses. Every effort is made, through auditions, to assure that each participant is placed at his or her appropriate skill level.

We are very proud of our teaching staff. All are well known and honored in the motion picture and television industries. Kim Darby, an Emmy and Golden Globe nominee — Joe Reich, a successful casting director for over thirty years, director of over a hundred plays in Los Angeles — Dee Wallace Stone, who has starred in many motion pictures and television movies — Mark Malis, television producer, formerly Vice President of Casting at Universal, who has cast over a thousand hours of prime time television — Joe Hacker, a USC professor with over 200 Class A National commercials, plus pilots,

Workshop Profiles

prime time TV shows, MOWs, feature films, etc., to his credit — Phil Ramuno, established TV Sit-Com director who has worked on hundreds of network and syndicated, comedies, starting with the legendary Soap, to Grace Under Fire — these and others will help you shape your skills and guide you through a successful career. Workshops are offered in Scene Study, Acting Technique, Advanced Cold Reading Technique, Soap Opera Intensives, Commercials, Acting on Camera, Screenwriting and our Casting Director Cold Reading series and our Agent Showcase. Workshops are designed to cover a variety of needs and will soon include Improv, Sitcom, Movement, Dialect and Voice-Over classes. To assure individual attention, all classes are limited to no more than twenty students, often less.

We believe in showcasing our talent. The positions held by our instructors in the theatrical community assure that our students are seen by those who can do them the most good: working professionals involved in the business of film and television.

We have one goal — to make you the best actor you can be.

Reel Pros
Hannah Sussman
Hannah Sussman is a professional working actress who put together a workshop for the professional working actor. Her husband is her partner. The workshops are geared to networking and being a gym for actors to work out. The audition process is carefully screened. This workshop serves the people who do the hiring, therefore increasing our participants' odds of getting parts. The concept here is to put the power back into the actor. Reel Pros will help you in strategically marketing yourself. You know what area of the business or type of show you should be seen for. They have a networking key that informs you as to whom you need to target, and see, in order to best present yourself. Once you've participated in one of their workshops, they keep a detailed actor record about you in their database. If a guest is casting a specific type, they perform a computerized search based on his criteria. If you fit, they will let you know that they submitted you. Your submission will have the advantage because your work was seen at his workshop or a general meeting at his office. Many actors ask, *"Why should I pay a casting person to see me act?"* They

answer; *"Because it's a business and industry guests, unfortunately, don't have time to go to 10-25 plays per month to find talent. They need to maximize their time, and so do you. You need a place where they can see you among 20 pros doing scenes that WORK YOU OUT! Hey, this is how thoroughbreds make it to the track."*

The Seenwork Company
Jeanette O'Connor
The Seenwork Company offers ongoing cold reading workshops for the professional actor with a different guest speaker each week. Regular nights are Thursdays at 7:30 and occasional Saturday afternoons are also scheduled. Membership is open to union members or by industry referral only. Auditions are by appointment. We'll also schedule periodic industry showcases with prepared scenes. This workshop is intended for educational and networking purposes only. Class fees range from $23 and up if there are multiple teachers. Recommended by casting directors, agents and managers. For more information, call 818 225 9851.

Terri Tunder Studios
Terri Tunder
Terri is the owner/operator of Terri Tunder Studios. Her actors take part in showcases every six to eight weeks for invited industry guests – except during pilot season. Terri directs all scenes and cold readings. For more information, call 213-683-3776 or 323-969-0795.

Show & Tell
Kylie Delre
At Show & Tell workshops, actors can expect to perform for and establish contacts with top casting directors, agents, and managers in a safe and exciting environment. Feedback and re-direction is encouraged from all the industry guests. Since an audition is required, actors can feel confident they will be performing with other dedicated and talented actors like themselves.

The workshops are designed to provide actors with the opportunity to meet and talk with industry professionals for approximately three hours, which include: Q & A, preparing cold reading materials from

MASTER THE ART OF COLD READING

specific projects, or prepared work (scenes and/or monologues) – dependent on the guests preference, and receiving feedback and/or applying re-direction to the work. Meeting the decision maker is the first step, keeping in touch and maintaining a professional working relationship is what is left up to you. Your agent only gets 10% for a reason. Don't walk into an audition as a means to an end – to get the job. Think of the part as yours, maybe for only five minutes; it is your opportunity to perform.

For an appointment or to inquire about the next audition times, call 818-759-7533. Show & Tell is located at THE ACTORS WORKOUT STUDIO, 4739 Lankershim Blvd. in North Hollywood.

Take One Studios

Take One Studios began operating in Los Angeles in 1990. T.J. Stein developed the company as a professional forum for actors to showcase their talent to top casting directors, agents, producers and directors. All actors must first audition to Take One Studios before being able to attend showcases. This policy ensures that we keep the level of talent to professional standards.

Each workshop begins with an introduction of the guest, questions and answers, followed by the presentation by the actors of the cold reading scenes provided by the guest. Take One Studios also offers on-camera soap and commercial workshops as well as three, four, and five week intensives for cold reading, scene study, monologue coaching, and mock casting!

Our professional atmosphere allows actors to take action in their career by networking with industry professionals. Take One Studios feels confident that the cold reading showcase forum is an excellent opportunity for actors to get to see casting directors, also reminds actors that when they attend workshop/showcases it is important to attend to grow as actors and not just to get a job!

TVI Actors Studio

TVI is a unique institution for actors, one that has been rapidly growing since 1986. With offices in Los Angeles and New York, a staff of thirty, and a teaching core of 35 industry professionals conducting classes, TVI is commanding the attention and respect of the entertainment industry.

Designed for the novice as well as the working actor, TVI stresses the business side of acting and the practical knowledge of today's marketplace in all its classes and workshops. TVI offers its students classes, seminars and workshops in which they interact with industry professionals such as casting directors, producers, directors and agents who then provide feedback as to what will enhance their employment opportunities. The classes fall under the category of: sitcoms, soaps, film, primetime TV, commercials, theatre, voice-overs and musical theatre. TVI also offers on-going cold reading workshops with casting directors and directors for as low as $12 for TVI members.

TVI starts with the basics, providing the actor with marketing: assistance and career counseling (i.e. resume and cover letter writing and up-to-date industry mailing labels). To its students, TVI also serves as a friendly and relaxed work-out-place where there are rehearsal halls and studio space equipped with cameras and lights.

You can see TVI students today working as series regulars on TV shows, contract roles on soap operas and leading parts in films, Broadway and commercials.

Van Mar Academy
Ivan Markota
The school opened with one professional student and membership increased steadily. It's a documented fact that 85% of our students who committed themselves to serious study have received SAG cards over the past ten years.

Ivan Markota's Van Mar Academy stresses cold readings, on-the-set-behavior, acting for the camera, and commercial hang-ups (things that might hinder you from getting a job). Ivan says: "I teach individually and take a personal interest in each and every person. I take my work seriously and excel in getting people rolling. I am a method-trained actor with a Master's Degree, but I don't stress the concepts, because I specialize in getting people to work, so I don't have the time needed for it. I feel that patience and perseverance as two of the most important qualifications an actor can have."

"I gave up a promising acting career and a $250,000 a year construction company that I had for fifteen years to devote myself to teaching. I thought that there was a need for what I had to offer." Some of the films I appeared in were Bob, Carol, Ted and Alice and Marooned. There is no business in the world (with the possible exception of espionage) that is as shrouded in myth, yesterday, and just plain B.S. as the motion picture and television industry. The similarities between becoming a professional spy and a professional screen actor are remarkable. So, if you are an actor in Hollywood trying to get your foot in the door, who do you turn to, who do you believe? Try Ivan Markota.

Weist-Barron-Hill
Our workshops have been designed to make you more successful at auditioning for and winning TV commercials, roles in soap operas, dramatic TV, sitcoms and film. What we don't offer are wild promises. Be wary of workshops that promise or intimate that they will be in a position to cast you after taking their workshop.

Casting directors cast actors with experience. So the most successful strategy to this business is to get solid training, learn your craft and polish your skills. And, in fact, part of our training includes showcasing our actors to the top agents and casting directors in the industry.

We're able to keep our tuition low because of the large numbers of classes we teach each week. Yet, each class is limited in size so that everyone receives individual attention on camera. The kind of direction, practice, and exposure offered in our commercial and acting workshops have made them the most effective in the country.

Weist-Barron-Hill, located at 4300 West Magnolia Blvd. in Burbank, offers classes in Commercials, Television, Soap Opera, Voice-Over, as well as classes specifically for Children and Teens and Agent and Casting Director Showcases. For more information, call 818-846-5595 or 818-880-5141.

WORKSHOP LISTINGS (partial listing)

Acting Workshop\Judy Pioli Askins	818-760-2428
AIA - Action in Acting www.aiastudios.com	818-563-4142
Act Now www.actnownetwork.com	818-840-2795
Actor's Edge	310-652-4399
Actorsite www.actorsite.com	310-787-6344 323-957-1159
AFTRA Casting Showcase	323-634-8262
David Goldyn's CD Workshops www.castingdirectorworkshops.com	818-988-PART
In The Act www.itaproductions.com	310-281-7772
One On One Productions www.oneononeproductions.com	818-789-3399
PrimeTime Actors Studio	213-874-4131
Reel Deal Showcase	818-771-8084
Reel Pros	818-788-4133
Seenwork seenwork@aol.com	818-225-9851
Show & Tell	818-759-7533
Aaron Speiser Acting Workshop www.aaronspeiser.com	310-399-4567
Take One Studios	310-390-6628

MASTER THE ART OF COLD READING

The Casting Break 818-990-9994
www.thecastingbreak.com

The Casting Connection 818-784-PART

The Casting Network 818-788-4792
www.thecastingnetwork.com

TVI 818-784-6500

Van Mar Academy 323-650-8823

Weist-Barron-Hill 818-846-5595

CHAPTER 3

NEW CD WORKSHOP GUIDELINES
Industry Commentaries
The widespread controversy surrounding cold reading workshops brought out many impassioned viewpoints. Here are two of them from industry professionals who were very vocal and hands-on during the many months of proceedings. I hope that they provide some valuable insight into the situation.
To view a copy of the Workshop Guidelines, visit www.laawc.com.

Gary M. Zuckerbrod
President, Casting Society Association
I had the privilege of meeting Mr. Zuckerbrod at his office on the Warner Bros. lot in Burbank, CA where he is currently casting *"Without A Trace"*, a 1 hour dramatic series for CBS. Mr. Zuckerbrod participated in the 8-10 month meeting process that determined the new guidelines for cold reading workshops. I asked him to comment on the agreement regarding the new operating guideline for casting director workshops. Here's what he had to say…

Gary Zuckerbrod: The guidelines are incredibly fair. They were well deliberated. Now if the state will take action to enforce them, these guidelines have the potential to eliminate illegitimate workshops. The CSA is not a policing organization, that is the state's responsibility. As president of CSA, I care about the ethics involved. A litigate workshop should have a casting director or approved casting associate teaching, imparting knowledge of audition techniques to actors with no promise of a job. This new agreement will decrease and in theory eliminate workshops that were strictly in business to make a buck and not to provide a valuable learning experience for actors. The biggest problem with workshops in the past was the lack of standardization. This is a first time agreement and we will have to wait to see how well it serves our community and then determine if it needs any adjustments.

Actors should not look at this agreement as full protection. All actors should contact their union, ask their advice and finally make their own determination, using the new guidelines, to decide if a workshop is right for them.

Cold reading workshops help to build up the actors skill level.

MASTER THE ART OF COLD READING

Artistic endeavors require honing. Think about it. There are seminars on how to interview for a regular 9-5 job. The cold reading audition is an actors entertainment job interview. The purpose of the workshops however is not a job interview. It's to practice and have an opportunity to learn from a casting director you respect. The reason we give head-shots back at the end of workshops now is because our City Attorney said keeping them may be misconstrued as a job interview.

The Casting Society Association has begun working with AFTRA & SAG to set up workshops and informational seminars that will help actors. We anticipate that these will start in the summer 2003.

Billy DaMota
Casting Director, CSA

I started my efforts to bring attention to the casting director workshop issue nearly 10 years ago. In the early 80s, as a casting director, I saw the workshops as a growing problem. Their intent and purpose was simple: to charge a fee to actors for the opportunity to meet and perform for working casting directors, and their staffs, for the purpose of securing employment on the shows and movies for which these casting professionals were engaged.

Over the years, I have brought the issue up with the Casting Society of America, The Screen Actors Guild, AFTRA, and the City Attorney's office. The CSA, which represents many of the casting directors involved with the workshop industry, did little to stop the abuse and exploitation. Half of their board members do workshops or who have staff members who do them, and there's even a workshop owner currently serving on their board. And SAG issued a resolution in May of last year, promising to do everything possible to protect its members, yet has not done anything to stop the continuing problem workshops represent to its membership with respect to paying for access. Last year, I was excited when the Division of Labor Standards Enforcement (part of the State of California Department of Labor) took upon the task of reviewing the issue, recognizing the legal problems inherent in the workshop industry, and addressing the issue with what ultimately became a Declaratory Judgment and guidelines by which many of these businesses would be required to operate.

CHAPTER 3

Except for a few cosmetic alterations to the workshop process, nothing has truly changed. The workshops are operating in much the same fashion they've operated for nearly two decades. The guidelines issued by the DLSE in November have been violated on dozens of occasions, and more importantly, the spirit of the guidelines have constantly been ignored. The effect of these guidelines should have been such that workshops would "change their ways" and offer strictly educational opportunities for actors. Instead of changing their business model to make education the only purpose for workshops, the state-issued Declaratory Judgment and the guidelines it includes have allowed most workshops to continue as they always have.

Here are some facts:
Every workshop continues to boldly advertise current casting projects in the workshop advertising. While this is not a violation of the guidelines per se, the manner in which these projects are advertised makes it clear what their service provides. Not one of the hundreds of "instructors" who have appeared in any of the workshops is NOT currently casting. Many of these workshops have violated the guidelines by either advertising their employment success rates on brag boards and Walls of Fame, by allowing guests to appear without a curriculum or lesson plan, by offering one-on-one general interviews with the casting director after performing, and by consistently advertising that workshops have a value other than that of an educational nature - which is strictly prohibited by the guidelines. Most workshops continue to offer what is essentially paid access.

I understand that this is a sticky issue. The workshops have spent oodles of money on attorneys to *"fight the state"*. They're a powerful, well-funded lobby. And I understand that many actors find workshops to be of great value in getting acting work. But the precedent which this cottage industry has set, and which it continues to promote is a dangerous one, one which hurts the majority of the actor workforce for the benefit of a handful.

In hundreds of e-mails and personal conversations with actors, I've heard the same thing over and over. These actors have been told by their friends, by their agents, and even by casting directors that to get more work - or sometimes any work - they should showcase their talent for casting directors in the any of the several casting director

New CD Workshop Guidelines

workshops in Los Angeles. This sad philosophy is reflected in statements made by top casting directors in Backstage West columnist Bonnie Gillespie's new book "Casting Q's".

* * * * * * * * * *

Cathy Henderson, CSA: *"Both Dori and I [attend] as many workshops as we can after a full day's work,"* Henderson said. *"I've seen some terrific actors in well-run, well-organized workshops. I'll bring them into the office based on the workshop experience. Dori and I have cast anywhere from 15 to 65% of non-star roles from workshops. Actors need to be ready before they do workshops for casting directors. It has a lot to do with the effort the actor puts into it,"* she qualified.

"Casting directors who don't work at studios or networks need a way to do general interviews more efficiently. From that, we already know what the actor is about, more than we would from a picture and resumé in a mailing. That's what the workshop is, for us. It's an amazingly wonderful way for actors to see casting directors who are working in an environment where phones aren't ringing off the hook."

Regarding the controversy of workshops as paid auditions: *"I always thought workshops were a good idea. Nobody twists the actor's arm to do it,"* she summarized. *"It's my job to do talent scouting. Workshops are just one of the ways I do that."*

* * * * * * * * * *

Michael Donovan, CSA, CCDA: *"The debate over workshops is outrageous. If you don't want to go, don't go. I recently hired a series regular from a workshop. It's a great opportunity. The general is a waste of time. I'd much rather see you audition for me, and not for a specific role as much as for the future. What does a mass mailing cost? $300? That's ten workshops. I would think you'd be better off getting your work in front of people instead of an ice cold envelope that may or may not get opened."*

* * * * * * * * * *

These are just two of several of such statements from the casting community. Both of these casting directors say *"Nobody twists the actor's arm to do it"* or *"If you don't want to go, don't go."* But it's not a "matter of choice" when at the same time, these casting directors, along with hundreds of others, use workshops on an increasing basis to find and hire actors.

To my best knowledge, the DLSE has done nothing to enforce the numerous violations of the guidelines, and it's not clear whether they ever intend to do so. Ultimately, it's actors who hold the key to ending a seemingly never-ending system of paying for access. The Screen Actors Guild's Section 47 states that every signatory producer must ensure that their casting directors provide at least one day per month of general interviews or attendance at SAG sponsored showcases. That's a lot of casting directors, and that's a lot of opportunity.

It's time actors stopped paying a casting assistant's rent when most have trouble paying their own. Actors comprise a community which is generally the least able to pay, yet they are compelled to pay and pay and pay in an effort to get their foot in the door.

In the big picture, completely eliminating the pay-for-access system which has become so acceptable in Los Angeles, and which has spread throughout the state and country in casting director related schemes, can only ultimately benefit the tens of thousands or artists who cannot - or will not - pay to be seen. Until actors demand that casting directors and their staffs stop being paid for a "service" which they are already paid quite well to do by their employers, then the system will never change. Until they demand that their union provide them with the opportunity they deserve, they will be relegated to paying for that opportunity.

FREE ALTERNATIVES

AFTRA Casting Showcase
The AFTRA Casting Showcase program is a free service that meets twice a month in the Boardroom of their Mid-Wilshire office. You and your partner must be paid up members of the Los Angeles local to participate. Only two person scenes are permitted. AFTRA cannot help you find a partner. Scenes may not exceed three minutes. No firearms or nudity will be permitted. Props must be kept simple and a table and chairs are provided. Call AFTRA to find out when the next showcase will be held. You will be given a day and a time span in which to call and register on a first come, first served basis. You must be ready with your social security number as well as your partners name and SS number.

SAG Agents Seminars

SAG Agents Seminars are held on the last Wednesday of every month. These seminars are primarily used as a forum to ask informational questions of the industry guests, not to solicit representation. They are held from 6:30 to 8:00 PM in the James Cagney Room at SAG headquarters. The seminar is free but seating is reserved and limited. To receive an invitation to the next seminar, write to Marilyn Rice at the SAG Committee Office, 5757 Wilshire Blvd. Los Angeles, CA 90036-3600. Be sure to include your name, address, phone number, and member ID or social security number.

CHAPTER FOUR
TIPS FROM INDUSTRY PROFESSIONALS

This section of the journal will provide you with advice and guidance. I've conducted a survey of industry professionals and asked the questions that will help actors give a winning cold reading.

Remember, a cold reading audition is an opportunity to show your talent and range as an actor. Try not to think of it as your last chance to become a star. Your job as an actor is to audition and perform memorable cold readings. Cold readings are an opportunity for you to meet industry professionals and for them to get to know you and all you have to offer. It's paying your dues. When you audition a lot, you can consider yourself a working actor in the sense that you are working on getting yourself known in the business. If you're not auditioning or cold reading, no one in the industry knows you exist. Here's what the industry has to say...

CASTING DIRECTORS

TERRY BERLAND
Here are a few tips and suggestions regarding cold reading. At the audition, there are usually instructions outside the room. Take a look around to find them. Also look to see if there is a storyboard posted and read that through.

Analyze your script. First figure out what the ad agency is doing to sell their product. A typical sell is through frustration or put down. Find your beats and moments. These are the places you have to apply your personality. I go in depth on how to do this in my six-week workshops. You should have a good idea who you are auditioning for. You'll have more confidence the more familiar you are with the entire process and the people on the other side of the camera.

For more information, contact Terry at (310) 571-4141 or tberland@aol.com. She is also the author of *"Breaking into Commercials: the complete guide to marketing yourself, auditioning to win, and getting the job"*.

MASTER THE ART OF COLD READING

MONA JACOBSON BREIER

As an actor pursues his or her career, invariably the cold reading/audition process will be an area that can be looked upon as an extremely " trying" experience, or as I like to look upon it, as a "challenging" part of an actor's pursuit.

With this in mind, I will attempt to mention a few of my own personal suggestions, when faced with a cold reading audition.

1. DON'T BE LATE. (My time is just as valuable as yours is. Traffic, car problems etc. are a natural part of life. Leave earlier.)

2. Always try to obtain the material as early as possible. Make use of modern technology such as your own fax machine, or the numerous outside "showbiz" fax companies.

3. When you enter a casting office, be sure to double/triple check that the sides you have are correct and the most revised for the role that you are auditioning for. I cannot begin to emphasize how important this is. Actors have come into my office unprepared for an audition with excuses as: " My agent only gave me a few pages off the fax", I didn't know what role I was reading for", etc. Just take those few minutes to review what is the most current material so you are adequately prepared.

4. Always bring a picture and resume to your auditions. Never assume that just because your agent set it up, that a picture arrived in time. (Keep a few in your car or briefcase for those last minute calls).

5. If you are unable to get the material ahead of time, try to arrive as early as possible to the audition, so you may have a few quiet minutes to review the material. If you need a few extra minutes, don't be afraid to ask the casting assistant if somebody else may go ahead of you. I'd much rather see you 5 or 10 minutes later than totally unprepared.

6. Energy and enthusiasm never hurts your audition and concentration on what you are doing will always serve you well. An actor in "daytime" should be prepared to concentrate under very tense and fast paced environments, as we tape a minimum of 5 shows per week.

Remember. Have fun and relax. YOU ARE AN ACTOR!

JAKI BROWN-KARMAN
An audition is the actors' moment. From the time the audition begins, all angst, stress and life's problems must be left outside the room. The entire focus should be on the audition. When it works it works and when it doesn't, you have left an impression.

CRAIG CAMPABASSO
As a casting director, I always make a conscious effort to calm nervous auditioners. One of my big sayings is; "Will you let fear rule you or let love guide the way?" I always try and keep that in my mind, because what a lot of actors are sensing all the time is that fear. I believe that the biggest mistake actors make when performing a cold reading is being nervous and forgetting that the casting director, producer and/or director are people like themselves. Most of all, that the actor chose acting as a profession for fun...So Have Fun With It! And just allow what comes from each acting experience. Let yourself become the character fully. This means that one must trust oneself completely.

Actors should prepare for cold readings by reading the full script, if possible. Research professionals behind the scenes. Ask yourself who is the character? How can I bring the role to life? Always go with your gut instinct. Research books, TV, movies and other characters similar to the one your are going up for. Again, trust yourself. Cold reading workshops are a good arena to grow as an artist and learn the profession from industry professionals. Actors should always keep in mind to use all the information they have gathered and use what is correct for them and their personality. There is no use making yourself crazy trying to please everyone. Try pleasing yourself for a change. Actors should stop taking cold reading workshops when they feel that they can completely surrender to the characters they are portraying. To not only be it, but to become it. I see the future of cold reading workshops becoming an even bigger arena of sharing ideas on acting techniques, applying them and most of all - to explore who the person is behind the actor. For if you do not know your true self, how can you portray all the other "selves" in the world?

MASTER THE ART OF COLD READING

When meeting with casting directors, producers or directors, walk into session fully in power. Make friendly eye contact and shake their hands and introduce yourself to everyone. Ask if there is anything you should know about the character before you start your reading. Once the reading is complete, ask if they would like to see it another way. If not, remember that they have been seeing countless other actors all day. You're a professional, so thank them, say your good-byes and exit. When you believe in yourself, others will believe in you! They will remember you, perhaps more so than all the others. When a part boils down to three or more choices, they are usually chosen by professionalism and how likeable they are.

LORI COBI

I am a casting director who believes the most common mistake actors make when giving a cold reading is that they don't ask questions. Actors need to get all the information they can get before they do a reading. Cold reading workshops help actors learn techniques and get feedback from casting directors. Actors should stop taking cold reading workshops when they are consistently getting call backs. I advise actors to study, ask questions, be prepared and try to relax.

CARA COSLOW

The most common mistakes actors make when giving a cold reading is talking too much - out of nerves. Actors need to take the sides home with them and work with someone. Get familiar with your cues. Cold reading workshops can be helpful to actors because a CD can take them through the complete process of cold reading. Actors should stop taking cold reading workshops when they are comfortable with the auditioning process. While you are in the workshop, be interested in what the CD has to say. You could learn something.

BILLY DAMOTA

Most actors are unprepared, have made no choices, have no character and get no work. Actors should always get material as soon as possible prior to audition and come in with strong choices. Cold reading workshops, with the right casting director can greatly help the actor to better understand the process and create familiarity with the industry people. Actors should stop taking cold reading workshops when they want to stop learning. Most cold reading workshops will continue to offer useful information to actors. I advise actors to do the work and don't ever give up.

TED HAHN
The most common mistake actors make when they cold read is that they rush. Actors should be willing to make mistakes. Cold reading workshops strengthen an actor's ability to be fearless. Cold reading workshops need to resize their classes. Frequently, there are just too many people in one class. I advise actors to take more time to listen to their partners. Don't worry, just do it!

HETTIE LYNNE HURTES
One of the biggest mistakes an actor makes when doing a reading, either a cold reading or a staged reading, is treating it as less important than a memorized scene. Actors tell me they're happy that they're ONLY doing a reading; that they don't need as much rehearsal time. WRONG! Even though it's not necessary to memorize a scene, it takes time and effort to develop your character and understand the motivation behind the scene. It's true that in a cold reading, an actor doesn't have a lot of time to develop a character; however, the casting director, agent or director is hoping to see how quickly you can create something believable. That takes focus and skill.

It's necessary to study cold reading techniques. Cold readings are a way of life in Hollywood. This is not a theatre town. It's a fast paced life of features, pilots and sitcoms. You often have only one chance to prove yourself. You'd better be prepared! If you can't afford to take a class in cold reading technique, you should read Master the Art of Cold Reading by Angel Harper and/or get together with fellow actors and form a workshop at which you can develop your skills, using one another as critics and guides.

As a casting director for Drama West Productions, I am most impressed by actors who take cold reading seriously and spend the time necessary to bring it to life.

MASTER THE ART OF COLD READING

SAM PANCAKE
As a casting assistant for commercial casting, I find that actors are too nervous, don't listen and are not "in the moment" by "not being present". To prepare for a cold reading, actors should be familiar with the "sides" as much as possible to have freedom of mind and control of the body. Know the show you are reading for! Cold reading workshops give actors good practice in a safe environment. The more an actor works on cold reading, the less nervous he will be. Nerves will stifle creativity. When you start booking jobs is time to stop taking cold reading workshops. My advice to actors is not to be nervous. Whatever it takes to get relaxed before an audition for you - get to that place. Be present and have fun! Don't have an "attitude." Nobody wants to work with an a****** - no matter how talented.

JAN POWELL
I have an extensive background in casting that spans over many years, covering the soaps, MOWs, features and television pilots. I find that the biggest mistake actors make when giving a cold reading is lack of concentration on the material and an unfocused character. Working in television, one must learn to be immediate. The actor is expected to present the character as fully developed as possible, whether anyone wants to admit it or not. Actors should concentrate on the printed word, forget props and blocking. We know what it's supposed to look like. We want to see as much of the character as possible, the emotional content and the fact that you can hold your concentration. Understand the character and the material.

Cold reading workshops are a benefit to actors, if for no other reason than it gives you a chance to practice with the pressure on. To find out what is really expected of you, so that each real casting session is just not another grope in the dark. Also, it gives you a chance to learn what different CDs expect. Actors should stop taking cold reading workshops when they get callbacks on a regular basis or begin to book jobs consistently. Then their skills are working. Especially, when you feel you are getting to the heart of the character in a short period of time.

I see the future of cold reading workshops with AFTRA and SAG hiring a staff to run them and hire the CDs to directly to teach them. Then, everyone will benefit to the utmost. My main advice to actors is to study and practice! Your education is never over. Learn about art, music, history, literature, quantum physics and welding - you get the idea. Everything helps us become the wonderful characters we hope to play someday. Become familiar with the great new theater repertoire as well as the classics and read everything aloud. Practice, practice, practice! Work out dramatically, intellectually, and physically. Keep a positive attitude and remember, it's just entertainment not brain surgery or a cure for cancer.

CLAIRE SINNETT

I have directed well over 50 stage productions. I am the founding Artistic Director of The Actors' Company Theater in Los Angeles. The audition process may be the most important factor in our business. What is an audition? It's a sharing of yourself-your thoughts, your feelings. Your "read", therefore, cannot be judged. Auditions should be fun. Remember, an audition is also the time the creativity belongs completely to the actor. After you're cast, it becomes the director's medium.

I believe that an actor's biggest mistake in performing a "winning" cold read is no eye contact. Read the material aloud so the sound of your own voice won't throw you. As long as the workshops are being taught by credible instructors and not just having the actors pay for the audition, cold reading workshops will be beneficial to actors. When you are working regularly, stop going. I see the future of cold reading workshops as credible directors teaching a five to eight week course. My advice to actors is to market themselves. It's the most important aspect of the business. The audition is the most creative part of the business.

PAMELA STATON

I have read two of the four editions of *Angel Harper's Master the Art of Cold Reading*. I not only recommend that EVERY actor should own a copy, but they should keep it in their car as a daily reference guide. As a casting director, I use many different methods for accomplishing my casting needs. The one skill that is essential to me, is in fact, the art of cold reading. When coming in for a cold reading, ask as many questions as you can about the character, the story, the other people involved. Begin accessing the situation at once and then let your

MASTER THE ART OF COLD READING

imagination take over from there. The words will suddenly have more meaning. Always know "who you are" in the scene. This mastered skill is the single element that separates the pros from the amateurs, and believe me it is evident. A masterful cold reader will undoubtedly get the job over someone less accomplished. Why? Because even after an actor is hired for a job, there will always be last minute changes to a script. Hence, you must be a skilled cold reader (quick thinker) simply to keep up. I will always push for someone with cold reading skills because that is what a director needs most.

A casting director needs skilled, prepared and dedicated actors to present to producers and directors. Develop a rapport with the casting director or their assistant and they will tell you everything you need to know. Remember, we are all doing a job and want to be our best.

An actor will find if they are a very good at improvisation, they will automatically have good cold reading skills. The two work hand in hand in that your mind stays sharp and creativity is more abundant.

LILA SELIK
Speaking as a casting director, cold readings are worthless! A prepared or even semi-prepared actor makes the audition run smoother and more professional. Giving the actor 2-3 hours with sides can make the difference between casting an actor that reads well and passing up somebody that will perform well throughout the production. When time permits, I will always provide an actor with sides, whether it be for commercial or theatrical. I once had an agent say to me: "Sides? For a 3-line commercial?" My reply was "Absolutely - the more information you give the actor, the better we both look!" In the audition it's the actor's performance on the line - nothing else! A bad performance on tape can do the actor far greater damage (it seems that everybody remembers a bad performance). Speaking as someone who started out in front of the cameras, I don't believe a cold reading can show the depth of actors or how far they can stretch their performances. If you have to read it cold, don't be afraid to ask the director/producer "How do you see the character?" (All you've wasted is 5 seconds of their time). However, make sure you can stretch your performance before asking this. In every case, if it's possible to pick up sides before the audition, DO IT!

Many times, you will be reading with a casting director, producer, or director. In my opinion, this is ridiculous! As a casting director, I personally would never object to any actor bringing a reader; and in most cases I highly recommend it!

AGENTS & MANAGERS

MELISA BIRNSTEIN
The most common mistake actors make when giving a cold read is that they don't focus on the material. That's why their choices tend to be weak. That's also why cold reading workshops are beneficial; they help actors know what to expect in a winning cold read. The workshops also help actors extract information that could help them for future auditions. Actors should meet a casting director only once at cold reading workshops. I see cold reading workshops expanding as a business. My advice to actors is to get a good team that to work for you and, on your own, go out and get some credits to back you up!

BROOKE BUNDY
The big mistake actors make when cold reading is that they don't have enough eye contact. They do not bring themselves into the role or they don't take risks. Relax and be confident. To prepare for a cold read, pick up your sides early. Get to know the material and have your own point of view. Cold reading workshops benefit actors because they give them immediate feedback. Once you book a series or a lead in a major feature, you don't need workshops anymore.

LEIGH GILBERT
One of the most common mistakes an actor makes when giving a cold reading is that they freeze up. Actors should practice and study cold reading, which is an oxymoron in itself. However, read out loud and listen to yourself. Cold reading workshops are an absolute necessity because they prepare the actor to understand and use their skills on the spot. Learn to trust your instincts.

MASTER THE ART OF COLD READING

RICK MARTEL
The most common mistake that actors make is trying to make an Academy Award performance out of the scene. Prepare yourself by making sure that your skills are very sharp. Cold reading workshops will allow you to meet casting directors and agents that you might otherwise never have had the opportunity to meet. Don't attend cold reading workshops when you finally realize that your skills are lacking. You don't want to leave a bad impression with the casting directors or agents for whom you perform.

JEREMY RITZER
I spent 22 years as a New York casting director. I began casting musical fairs in 1966 and switched my casting direction in 1970 to commercials, while working for Doyle Dane Bernbach and McCann-Erickson Advertising. In 1975, I went into partnership with Howard Feuer and for 10 years, cast movies, television, and theater. Among our projects: Fame, Hair, Places in the Heart, All That Jazz, and Star '80. I also helped put together the original cast of L.A. LAW. As for cold readings, block out all distractions and think only of the immediacy of the character. I recommend that actors allow themselves enough time to study your lines. You don't prepare for a cold reading - you just do it! If you are smart enough to take time to prepare, your never have to "cold" read.

TEACHERS & COACHES

Ron Burrus Acting Studio
Ron Burrus
This tip is for the actor just beginning to acquire cold reading skills:
1. Read out loud for 10 minutes straight everyday for two weeks - material can be anything around the house (newspaper - magazines).

2. As you continue to do the above, read out loud the SENSE of what is written - no acting - just allow yourself to find the SENSE of it as you pick the material up cold without pre-reading it.

3. Now, send that sense of what is written to a spot outside of you (the doorknob, window, picture on the wall) - no mirrors, please.

4. The eyes, sense of the text and the spoken words are all going in one direction - off the page to the spot away from you and not back to the page. This is a coordinated effort that involves many muscles and they will all work together through practice.

From The Heart Acting Studios
Phil Esposito

First and foremost, the actor must cold read as often as possible. It is a muscle that needs to be worked and the more it is, the stronger it gets, like any other muscle. As you get better at it, your confidence grows and eventually that shows and you get the job! My classes are fifty per cent cold reading and fifty per cent memorized work. As an actor myself, I know that you never get to do the memorized work if you can't do the cold reading.

The rest of my technique has everything to do with why my studio is called From the Heart. Every one of us has something unique and special, something that makes us who we are and how we are perceived. Most actors, when given a few pages of dialogue, tend to throw that out the window. They come from their heads and figure out what everyone else has figured out and basically give the same reading as everyone else. I ask my students to bring themselves to the work, regardless of logic, and in that way stand out at their auditions. If you laugh at funerals and cry at parades, then that's who you are and the energy required stifling that simply makes you come across as false. They may not like what they see but they will know that they saw the truth. It doesn't always get you the job that you are reading for but it does get you their attention and maybe another opportunity down the line.

Alan Feinstein/Paul Tuerpe Acting Studio
Alan Feinstein

True cold reading means you do not read the script in advance. You just turn it over and go. I find this frees the actor from preconceived judgements and allows their talent and imagination to just soar.

MASTER THE ART OF COLD READING

Ellen Gerstein's Acting Studio
Ellen Gerstein

The very first thing for the actor to do is to read the material several times and understand the story line. Script analysis is the key to specific acting. If you are general or if you are just saying lines well, that is not good enough. You must really understand every color, beat and transition, and make the material unforgettable. The actor must make the scene real to them. Of course when you do this, your confidence is high, which makes for your best audition.

There are some technical tips on holding the sides and going to the sides and coming off of it quickly, so you will have the maximum contact with your partner. Always remember, every moment is the only moment and do not anticipate. Of course, walk in confidently, and most importantly, have fun. If you do, they will.

To The Top Entertainment, An Actors' & Artists' Network
Jay Peter Hastings

Jay believes it is important to treat everyone nicely at cold reading workshops. "You don't know who is going to be doing what tomorrow. One of your fellow actors could become a director or producer. A lot of people get breaks from cold reading workshops. That's why they can be a vital part of marketing oneself."

At To The Top, we like to work with independent producers, directors, and writers. It is smart to meet people on the way up. Many of our actors work in independent films. My tip on cold reading is: Don't worry about the results or pleasing the casting director or industry professional at the workshop. Focus on becoming the character. I find it's the people that don't care about impressing anyone that do the best reading and get the jobs.

For more information, contact them at www.tothetop.net.

Weist-Barron-Hill
Dr. Andrea Hill

A good cold reading is fifty per cent what the writer intended and fifty per cent the actor's creation. It's about finding the purpose and meaning of the scene quickly. Don't be afraid to search for the deepest subtext for each line and then go beyond that to express your own personal contribution. Have the courage to show as much range as the scene allows and always read as truthfully and believably as you can. Create a life for your character that begins before the scene starts and continues after the scene is finished. Imagine your scene as a few moments in someone's life. Then live those few moments as the character.

Richard Kline
Writer, Comedy Coach
Assuming you are prepared with the basics (What is a relationship? What am I after and what is preventing me from getting it?), be aware of what "playing field" you're on. In other words, if it is a sit-com, make sure the energy level is appropriate to that medium. Locate and clarify the jokes. That's what the writer/producer is looking for. If it is a soap, the energy and focus will be different. If it's a WB show, give them that performance level. Whether it's The Young and the Restless or The Practice – give them a reading consistent with those shows. And remember you are only as good as the relationship you establish in the reading with the casting director. Some read better than others, no matter. You have to establish a relationship between your character and the one the casting person is reading to create any sense of "in the moment" acting.

Millie Slavin
Teacher, Coach
The single most important factor that empowers an actor to consistently deliver exciting cold readings is having learned a solid craft. I believe this approach will never let the actor down. A successful cold reading requires more than just talent. The actor must be able to put that talent to use intuitively and at a moment's notice. That skill comes only with diligent study and disciplined practice of the basic arts of acting. Those arts can then become deeply ingrained into the actor's responses.

Experience has taught me that cold reading workshops as a primary learning technique are insufficient preparation for the inexperienced and untrained, and can lead to "hit or miss" results in the actual cold reading setting. An actor who hasn't developed his craft through

MASTER THE ART OF COLD READING

training cannot expect to consistently translate the skills he might learn from the workshop to the audition. Without such a foundation, cold reading classes alone may lead the actor into non-productive habits or patterns. Having said that, cold reading techniques taught by skilled professionals as part of your overall study plan can greatly enhance your ability to secure acting roles.

There is one crucial thing to remember at a cold reading: retain your balance and keep a cheerful, cooperative attitude if asked to make an "on your feet" adjustment. Occasionally, adjustments will be requested, merely to test the actor's ability and willingness to branch out and exhibit flexibility. View it as a challenge, not an imposition or a chore.

Ms. Slavin, a Cable Ace Award Nominee, has received numerous accolades from professionals in the industry. She offers private coaching and small scene study classes that include cold reading techniques. For information, call (310) 582-3485.

DIRECTORS

MICHAEL ARABIAN

I had been an actor for ten years in both New York and Los Angeles. I trained at Webber Douglas Academy of Dramatic Art in London, under a full scholarship. I have performed at such theater companies as the Mark Taper Forum, L.A. Theatre Works and Playwrights Horizons. I have also appeared in numerous television and film roles. I was the recipient of a 1979 Villager Award in New York and three Drama-Logue awards in Los Angeles. I started directing and producing full-time some years ago in Los Angeles with four critically acclaimed west coast premieres including: Request Concert, Scenes From American Life, Found A Peanut, Phantom Limbs, and Spring Awakening. These productions received a total of 18 Drama-Logue awards and five L.A. Weekly awards.

I find that actors either underplay or overplay in a cold reading. Basically, they are "acting" rather than expressing in the normal way they would express. Actors are concerned about the style of the character rather than the truth. Actors should never do a cold reading. You have the right to ask for the material ahead of time. Never look at the material in the office. Step outside. Rehearse your reading as you would any part. Do a character breakdown, history, relationship to other characters. Think about the situation. Make strong choices. Learn to take the reading off the page and focus on the other actor.

Cold reading workshops gives an actor practice and practice makes perfect. Actors should stop taking workshops when they start to stagnate. There is only so much you can learn doing cold reading workshops. If you are auditioning a lot, you don't need to do cold reading workshops as much. As long as the auditioning process is the way it is, cold reading workshops will always be useful. I advise actors not to take cold reading workshops as a substitute for an acting class. It's a specific technique.

RACHEL FELDMAN

I was a child actress. I have directed Doogie Howser and Post Modern Romance for HBO. My film credits include Witchcraft III. I believe that the actor's biggest mistake in giving a cold reading is not directing their attention to the work. They spend more energy on small talk and trying to get everyone to warm up to them rather than focusing on relaxing and performing. To prepare for a cold read, actors should read the "sides" over and over. Try to understand what the scene is about and how your character fits into it. Go for the obvious first.

JOEL ROSENZWEIG

One of the biggest mistakes an actor can make during a cold reading is to allow the person that they are reading with to change their interpretation of the character. To prepare for the reading, identify one line that the character says with one that you always say and from that aspect, you can personalize the script.

It is the young (new) actor's primary job to meet the people who are working in the industry. That's why cold reading workshops are so valuable to the actor. Don't stop until you have seen everyone on the schedule within the last eighteen months. Hopefully, more producers, directors, writers (and fewer casting directors) will conduct cold reading workshops. This will aid those who don't meet enough new talent. I'd like to advise actors to develop a mailing list. Personalize your cards and letters and find unique reasons for your mailings.

PRODUCERS

CARL CRAIG

I am a self-taught producer. My accomplishments include four HBO specials for Robert Townsend's Partners In Crime, for which I won an ACE Award for Best Producer, as well as Hollywood Shuffle and Mo' Money. I have observed that most actors don't ask questions regarding their characters' personality and relationship. Actors should prepare for a cold reading by learning as much of the dialogue as possible and then be very loose. Also, come in to the audition as close to character as possible. Cold reading workshops are good to take to keep an actor loose. I advise actors to ask who and what role they are playing. Know as much as possible about the situation. Then, in your reading, add something else to the dialogue that would make your character different. Remember, we hear the same lines over and over!

B J. FOSTER

Acting can be such a mystery at times because getting the job rests on so many factors other than the ability to act. But as an actress and a producer I've come to learn what I wish I had learned years before: whatever you do, do it boldly. Having worked in the industry for over twenty years, I honestly never knew what got me the job over someone else. Let's face it, there's always someone else just as talented, just as pretty, or just as charismatic. So what's the advantage? Choices! I can not stress how many talented actors I auditioned who did not get the part because they failed to take a solid stance on something. I would rather a bold choice that's totally wrong for the character, than no choice at all. At least I will remember that person and will call them again for something else. If that person will make choices for themselves, then they will make choices for me. As a producer, that actor is a gold mine!

CHAPTER 4

ANN MARIE GILLEN

I produced Fried Green Tomatoes. I believe that most actors are not prepared and socialize with everyone. It's important to focus. Actors should come early and get the sides and study the breakdown by beats and emotions. Rehearse-Rehearse-Rehearse, until the audition. Cold reading workshops give you technical skills. For example; think about holding the script, who should you act to, to use or not to use props, your mental focus and just knowing how to meet a casting director. You should stop taking cold reading workshops when you are not learning anything. Actors should get out of the business unless it's the only thing you want to do. Actors need to have hobbies or volunteer jobs to balance their life. It helps you become an interesting person so you can discuss something other than your agent or next job.

JAMES B. LAVERT

The biggest mistake many actors make when giving a cold reading is thinking that there is something called "cold reading." Talent is never "cold." Many of an actor's best moments come when the material is fresh. Inspiration is a misnomer. Those unique moments seem to come out of nowhere are talent in its purest form. Be willing to discover which direction your talent wants to take you. This defies all logic, which precisely the point since logic is the antithesis of creativity! Trust your talent! The best preparation is learning to read quickly from a page so that your focus and attention is always on the other actor or person you are reading with. Charles Conrad prescribed practicing a minimum of three times a day, four minutes a session. Pick a spot on the wall, hold the script/book etc. chest high, glance down briefly, pick a few words, instantly look back at the spot on the wall and speak the dialogue/words. After a period of time you should be able to pick up whole sentences with just a flick of the eye on the page. Without your head buried in the script at a reading, you begin to look and respond as a creative person.

Cold reading workshops benefit actors because it gives them practice! In most cases, forget what the person heading the workshop says to you. You should have already learned your craft with a master of acting and are now using the workshop to meet people and practice reading from the varied and usually lousy material. You should stop taking cold reading workshops when you are working regularly or just get sick of them. I don't have a vision for the future of cold reading workshops, but if I did it might be that they become a place of honest evaluation for the actor and the host. A place where everyone looks to discover the wonderful things that will be exposed through talent. Don't settle for anything less than complete use of your creative powers.

PATRICIA K. MEYER

I produced the Emmy-nominated ABC miniseries, The Women of Brewster Place, based on the novel I optioned. The film, starring Oprah Winfrey, was a co-production with Phoenix (now Hearst) Entertainment and Harpo Productions. It aired in March 1989, with top ratings. In December, I was Executive Consultant on the series, Brewster Place, which aired on ABC in the fall of 1990. I also produced a CBS movie, Menu for Murder. My first motion picture was released by FOX in February '92, entitled This Is My Life. I served as Executive Producer.

Actors tend to overact and are too nervous. They also have a bias attitude. There is a fine line between coming on too strong and not being animated enough. Actors should prepare for a cold reading by relaxing. Think about the role. Consider what kind of movie it is. Cold reading workshops help actors prepare for spontaneity. Learn to improv. When you start getting regular work, stop taking cold reading workshops. Actors should keep pushing their agents to put them up for roles. Be aware of up-coming auditions. Be your natural self as much as you can. When performing cold readings, relax and work hard!

MARIE ROWE

As Associate Producer on many of Barry Levinson's films, I have worked closely with him on the writing of several of his screenplays and in casting on most of his feature films he has directed. He always emphasizes "less is more," and encourages actors to relax into the character and let go of the effort.

I appreciate the actor who has the courage to break away from the written material in a cold reading and go beyond the character as written - to improvise. Of course, this requires a complete understanding of the material, not just the lines but the whole scene in which the character appears. I'm disappointed when an actor fails to fully absorb the scene he's asked to read. I also prefer that actors memorize their lines as much as possible, and I am strongly opposed to the clutching of sides as a security tactic. I believe that releasing lines to memory sets free the essence of the character, allowing for more flexibility.

Cold reading workshops can still instill confidence in the actor - allow more freedom and expression of character, therefore avoiding the rigidity of being locked into the words. In my opinion, once this confidence is attained, then there's no more need for cold reading workshops.

CARMEN H. SETSON
As a member of the Ensemble Studio West, I produced Colors, An Anthem to Cultural Friendship, Paul Robeson, and West Memphis Mojo. I produced the Gala Finals for the Fifth Annual Ira Aldridge Acting Awards at the Beverly Theater, and the Evening of One-Acts for the Los Angeles Black Playwrights at the Westwood Playhouse. There is no such thing as a cold reading that is successful! Actors need to know the circumstances of the scene. Familiarize yourself with the environment. Determine beats. Make a tag. Cold reading workshops are good for practice. Practice makes perfect. Feedback is essential. I see cold reading workshops becoming totally technological (video and computer). I advise actors to never stop if you love it.

ACTORSPEAK

This section will give you an overview of what actors like yourself have experienced with cold reading workshops. I hope you will be enriched and inspired to jot down some of your own thoughts on the subject as you read the testimonials from other actors. Please send your testimonial to me and you may be included in the next revision of this journal. Together, we can take away the mystery and fear of how to give a winning cold reading.

MASTER THE ART OF COLD READING

MAURIZIO BARRA

Cold reading workshops are beneficial only if the actor knows how to cold read, if not, he/she should train first and get familiar with the process. One of the most common mistakes I feel actors make is in not trusting his or her memory, therefore their eyes are glued to the paper most of the time and therefore the spontaneity of the moment fades. They can overcome this problem by either sitting in front of a mirror, a person, or an object and gradually read as much text as possible without continually going back and forth from the page to whatever it is you are communicating with. In doing this, the eye gets trained and soon it will be able to "catch" lines at a time.

ADILAH BARNES

Many things I've learned over my 27+ years of acting have come to me by trial and error. I now apply what I've learned for myself and the numerous students I've taught over the last 15 years.

In my years as a working actress in Los Angeles, I've rarely had a true "cold reading." If not the entire script, more often than not I have sides before my scheduled audition time. Therefore, my auditioning ritual is generally the same whether I've prepared extensively before reading or not. I first read the material to get a good understanding of the script, such as given circumstances, character and relationships. I highlight my lines with a colored marker and my cue lines in a contrasting color. I mark beats and underline operative words. My sides often times look like sheet music!

Before entering that ominous room, I find a quiet corner or hallway to prepare. I acknowledge others I know that may be auditioning, but no socializing for me. My mission is to land the part. Once settled, I read aloud to hear my own voice. I also visualize myself entering the room with powerful, focused and relaxed energy. I claim my personal power before entering the room and strive to maintain it until I exit.

Once inside, I try to greet the casting team sincerely. I listen to the person reading with me and make regular eye contact. Above all, I try to enjoy the audition! I dress suggestively and try to give a strong closure to the reading and my interaction with the casting team. I make direct eye contact entering and exiting. I try never to let them see me sweat!

Most importantly, if I really want the role and believe I'm capable, I maintain that belief and affirmation every step of the auditioning process - including a written affirmation on one of my mirrors at home!

JULIE BREIHAN

Read continually – out loud – to keep your face muscles conditioned. If you read and understand what you're reading, it's more than likely that if someone were listening to you, they would understand also. Too often in an audition, the main criticism is that the director has no idea who you're talking to.

BERNIE CASEY

I made my film debut in Guns of the Magnificent Seven. A series of films followed such as Never Say Never Again with Sean Connery and I'm Gonna Get You Sucka, to name a few. I believe the most common mistake actors make in a cold reading is forgetting it's a reading and not a performance. I advise that actors are better served reading and not performing. Some casting directors prefer you to be off book but there is a danger in that! When reading, leave room for interpretation by the person listening to you. Be mindful of what time of day it is. Don't waste their time. It can backfire on you. Also, know that the five minutes you are getting is yours. Don't come in shy or non-aggressive. Come in and fill the room with your presence. Be forceful and memorable, remember the producer, director, and casting director is there. If you are not right for the role you're reading, you may be cast for something else. Know that most casting directors and producers have an image of the character, so when you walk in they know right away if its not you. Don't take it personally!!! It's important not to dress for the role too literally. Be in the realm of possibility. Be in the rhythm of the role. Be courteous and polite.

TORY CHRISTOPHER

Do your homework. Know to the CDs credits so you can ask intelligent questions. Respect your fellow actors during readings. Work together. Don't compete for the CDs attention.

E. VICKI ELLIS

I believe that actors should keep studying - just to keep in shape. The biggest mistake actors make in a cold reading is not creating what has come before in the scene or what will come after, such as relationships to other characters. Actors should prepare for a cold reading by reading through the sides. Clear other thoughts from your mind and don't let the audition distract you. A cold reading measures the actor's ability to take the words off the page and discover whether the choices you make for the character are good.

ANNE FAIRUE
I have been doing Take One cold reading showcases for over a year. This is one of the ways that I choose to spend the money I put into promoting myself. After about four months, I started getting work. In one nine-month period, I booked ten jobs. Six were the direct results of the showcases. Three were a direct result of the techniques and confidence I gained working with one casting director that I used later in auditioning for another.

KAROLTE FOREMAN
I believe that actors don't listen, don't make strong choices or follow through. Actors should prepare for a cold reading by centering themselves. Read through the "sides" looking for clues to the character. Then ask; Who? What? Where? Why? Cold reading workshops are a benefit to actors because they help to improve their craft and make you a better cold reader. Actors should never stop taking workshops.

JAMES GORE
One of the great benefits of attending cold reading workshops is that you get accustomed to getting fresh sides and learning how to make solid choices and committing to those choices to be able to perform and deliver a strong read. You should check around and audit classes and work in different workshops and get a lot of different feedback from actors and casting directors that you know and trust. It just creates a comfort zone for you, makes your performance stronger.

JANA LEVENSTEIN
It's good to buy into cold reading workshops and just plow through

them. That way you get some momentum going. It's an excellent way to keep your activity up, and then if you happen to do a great job, the right person to see you is right there. Sometimes you don't hear anything for a while and then, miraculously, you get a call.

JOHN FORD McCORMICK
Basically it's a two-step process in cold reading. You can't be good in cold reading unless you take a cold reading workshop and a cold reading workshop is important so you learn the art of cold reading, which every single audition is based on. And the second best part about cold reading workshops is that you get to meet casting directors who are working on projects who then in turn will cast you when you have mastered the art of cold reading. I've taken several and through a class with Gail Camacho, I booked work on The Young and The Restless and then I spent three months on Days of Our Lives through a class with Linda Poindexter. Talent has something to do with it, but you also have to know the right people and make them aware of you in return.

DAVID McKNIGHT
I was nominated for a 1991 NAACP Theater Award for my role in Soldiers and may be best known for co-starring in Robert Townsend's Hollywood Shuffle. The biggest mistake that actors make when giving a cold reading is they fail to realize that the scene must be analyzed to a point of understanding a point of view. Actors should relax, concentrate and read the words out loud. All workshops are beneficial in developing the actor's instrument and craft. Realize that you are in business for yourself! They're human and they will respond. Don't be afraid to ask to start over - it's not life or death and it's not brain surgery. It Is Your 5 Minute Audition!!!

ERIC MILES
I've found three basic things that can be said about workshops in LA. First, they are a long-term investment in career development, sometimes taking up to a year before returning a dividend. Second, many actors don't understand how the format and forum are designed. Third, if you approach them correctly, cold reading workshops can pay off abundantly. The problem is that many actors

have a misconception concerning the purpose of cold reading workshops. The cold reading workshop is not, I repeat, not a cold reading class. If you want to learn the technique of effective cold reading, TAKE A CLASS.

SAUNDRA SHARP

Actors don't take time to actually read the material and make choices before starting to audition. Listen to the director and focus on what he/she wants.

ELIZABETH SHE

Actors don't take enough time to center their thoughts before they start to read. Take a deep breath and relax. Don't stare at the page and just read off it. Relax. Look at the words. Look up, have eye contact and go for it! Practice makes perfect.

CARL BANKS SMITH

Actors don't allow their experiences to take over at any given moment because of predetermined choices and/or ideas. They commit themselves to their first impression of how they feel a part should play and look. Look at a part and see if there are any stumbling blocks such as difficult to read pronunciations. Get yourself exposure to casting directors at cold reading workshops. Don't stop taking them until the scripts are being delivered to your door. Be persistent. Have patience. Keep your energy up. You can't afford the luxury of a negative thought.

PATTY TOSSY

As an actress, I believe there are two common mistakes actors make when giving a cold reading. First, burdening themselves with trying to memorize the lines. They have the script in their hands, so use it. Why add to the pressure of the moment by trying to learn lines? Second, trying to second-guess what the auditioners want. Most of the time, they want the actor to show them something unique, so give it to them - YOU!!! The best way to prepare for a cold reading is to stay relaxed, so that you are open to your impulses. If it's a true cold reading (that is, you have had NO chance to study it), all the actor can do is stay loose. If you are given a few minutes to look it over, first digest the gist of the scene. Then decide on one objective and stay with that choice. Don't switch objectives in mid-stream. Cold reading workshops are a benefit to actors because they give you a chance to practice under pressure. It's also a one-on-one meeting with an industry professional that you might never have a chance to meet otherwise. Additionally, it's a wonderful chance to interact with other actors. Basically, actors should never stop taking cold reading workshops. But, if you are going to stop, do it when you are working steadily. At least then you're "on the boards" practicing your craft. The important thing is to keep the creative juices flowing, so, do workshops in between jobs, at least. Cold reading workshops are going to become big business. I hate paying to meet a casting director, but at least there's the possibility of work from their getting to know me.

DALE E. TURNER
My ability to listen and share during a cold reading granted me success with several different CDs and directors over the years. You have to be willing to share time with each other. Too many actors become so involved with what they're doing that they've forgotten the other person that they're dealing with!

ACADEMIA

Over the years I have inquired about how theater arts programs in colleges and universities deal with cold reading. I did major in performing arts at Cornell University. I assumed that since then, auditioning techniques were taught as part of a BA program but they are not. During my research I was fortunate to get a few of the professors to comment on the lack of cold reading training in the academic arena. Here's what they had to say...

DR. DONALD HAYES
Chairman L.A. Valley College Theatre Arts Dept.
In the summer of 1994, I had the privilege of meeting Angel Harper while she was in rehearsal for the play Julius Caesar at Los Angeles Valley College. It was not long before I discovered she was not a self-

MASTER THE ART OF COLD READING

absorbed actress. This book, Master the Art of Cold Reading, is an extension of her desire to give back to an industry she loves. Until I read the book, it had not occurred to me that the subject of cold reading is not taught as a separate subject for Theatre Arts majors. Learning how to cold read is the secret ingredient to getting work in Hollywood. However, solid acting skills will keep you working.

All actors need to make themselves aware of cold reading techniques. Believe me, when I look out on the market and see what's available, be it in books, videos, tapes or seminars, the offering is very scant. A tenured professor in Theatre Arts with over twenty years of experience, as well as a working actor, I highly endorsed Angel Harper's book and seminar.

You will benefit from Angel's seminar and/or book, regardless of what phase your acting career is at. I applaud Angel for this contribution. I wish you, the reader, much success.

BRUCE LEVITT
Department Of Theatre Arts, Cornell University
Every profession demands of its practitioners a basic skill, the knowledge and execution of which is fundamental in the pursuit of a job within that given profession. In the theatre that basic skill is the audition. However, in the past decade or so, the kind of audition and the skill required has slowly evolved away from the prepared reading to the cold reading.

A decade ago or so the prepared audition where the actor memorized monologues and presented them to casting directors, film directors and stage directors, was used much more frequently. Today, prepared auditions for the most part are used in only two instances: when someone auditions for a graduate school or when an actor auditions for a long term residency within a company of actors who are all expected to play within several productions and where the director wants to see range in the actor. For the most part today however, the cold reading is the standard entry level skill needed by every actor. There are two kinds of situations that pertain to cold readings. The first is when the actor arrives at an audition and is given a "side," or a copy of a script with certain pages marked to look over and then within a certain limited period is called into the audition space to read the text. The second cold reading allows the actor a bit more time. Some casting, film, and theatre directors are thoughtful enough to allow actors to pick up sides or scripts a day or two before the reading and to read over the scene or script for which the actor is auditioning. While the second kind of cold reading allows more preparation time, it still requires some of the same skills as the virtually on the spot reading required in the first instance.

The skills required include an ability to analyze a text quickly, to make strong appropriate choices about the character and the character's intentions, and to execute those choices in a full and compelling manner, often in less than ideal physical surroundings.

While an actor may be the most appropriate person for a given role, if the cold reading skills are unable to demonstrate the actor's appropriateness, then the actor is not going to get cast. It is imperative then for anyone who wants to pursue acting as a career to work on the skill of cold reading which has a special set of techniques that are separate and apart from the work one normally does on a role and sometimes, depending on the actor's training, can seem foreign to that process.

Cornell University: 430 College Avenue, Ithaca, NY 14850-4696 (607) 254-2700

LEE BOGGUS KNIPPENBERG
Director Of Theatre, Oglethorpe University
As a teacher and director, I use cold readings regularly with my students, both in the classroom and when auditioning for shows. I find that students want to rely too heavily on their prepared pieces, and this traps their creativity and forces it to flow in certain predisposed patterns. Encouraging students to read cold forces them to think on their feet and work in the moment. I always tell my students to eliminate one word from their vocabulary when approaching a script cold. The word is no. Once that has been eliminated, anything is possible. As an actress, I find cold readings exhilarating. That unknown element added to the audition process places an edge of excitement on the audition that keeps me focused. I enjoy the freedom found in the immediacy of the moment.

Lee Boggus Knippenberg received her B.A. from Oglethorpe University, her MFA from the University of Georgia, and is a graduate of the American Conservatory Theatre's Summer Training Congress. She has worked professionally in theatre for the past ten years. Since 1990 she has been Director of Theatre at Oglethorpe University in Atlanta, Georgia. Oglethorpe University: 4484 Peachtree Road, Atlanta, Georgia 30319 (404) 261-1441.

GREGORY B. ABBOTT
Artistic Director,
Dramatech Theater, Georgia Institute Of Technology
My Advice Concerning Cold Readings:
-Study: Classes, workshops actual auditions and books such as this one are invaluable.
-Know what you are auditioning for, get as familiar with the material as possible in the time available.
-Learn how to calm your nerves so you are free to act and react.
-Above all, make bold (but not stupid) choices.

The competition is fierce and will continue to be so. An actor's salvation is often his/her imagination,
judgement and confidence.

Georgia Institute of Technology: The Ivan Allen College, School of Literature, Communication and Culture, Atlanta, Georgia (404) 894-894-2730.

CHAPTER FIVE
COLD READING FOR THE YOUNG ACTOR

Class Act...The Young Actor's Studio
Jeff Alan
The most important thing you can so at an audition and cold reading is to trust yourself. You, in and of yourself, are enough. There is no one else like you and that is what we pay money to see. Make the script real and personal. Find similarities between yourself and the character and add to the mix that one wonderful thing that only you can do.

Toni Atell
Teacher
For adult actors, children and teen actors and interested parties in the cold reading process I would like to say" Congratulations and may you have Great Success!" Cold reading technique is a bit different from acting because it simply is what it implies. A cold read. For actors who are usually consummate in what they do, this can be a bit odd at first, since preparation should not be overdone and kept fresh. Basic rules are: Look, Listen, and Respond. Please, if I can offer this suggestion: LESS IS MORE!

Remember that a cold read is all they are asking for. The casting director, producer and director, usually want a simple read that they can work with and help shape. However, some casting directors who cast weekly shows have said just the opposite and claim the director doesn't have time to shape anything but the show. They recommend the actor come totally prepared with all their choices for the character as if they were walking right from the casting office onto the set.

My own personal observations are that you need to study not only which show you are cold reading for but the style of the show and what the individual casting directors' preferences are for that shows cold read.

Cold reading workshops are a good tool for this information as well an agent or managers feedback on the individual style of the casting director. Remember the casting director is on your side, they want you to get the job. Trust your choices and remember your first choice is usually the best choice. A good rule of thumb to remember is that the casting director has chosen you from your picture and so they know that you already have the look they want for their project. Congratulations on that! So using who you are, start to make choices of your backlife and the characters' (your) choices. Specific choices and attitudes work well. I find working with intentions and colors also help for the cold read and auditions. Bring no props and keep costuming to very little if any and use your rehearsal time for just that. Remember to drop all rehearsal stuff before you walk into the office and just relax and have fun, knowing that your instrument will remember what you have rehearsed. Good luck and remember you are more than enough!

Michelle Dahlin's Theatrical Workshop for Young Actors
Michelle Dahlin

In her several years as a working actress and assistant agent in Los Angeles, Michelle has had the opportunity to work with many child actors. From her experiences, she has discovered the importance of audition and cold reading techniques for young actors. Michelle, who has a Bachelor Degree in Dramatic Art from the University of California, Irvine, uses her extensive background to enhance and refine those techniques with her students.

The audition is the most difficult and unnatural experience any actor will face. My class focus is on making this daunting process successful, and even exciting! I employ the use of many theater games, improvisations, and scene studies to make learning technique fun and entertaining.

One of my favorite exercises to do with my students involves role-playing. Two students choose a new scene and are given ten minutes to work on it. When they return, they pretend they are stepping into a real casting session and meeting the casting director, writer, producer, and director, played by the other students. This teaches the students that the audition is not only about reading their script, but also about walking into that room and conducting themselves like professional actors. My students love this exercise because they can apply it directly to their own careers. It gives them power and confidence because they know more what to expect going into an audition.

Another vital aspect of my class is the presence of my students' parents. If the child is in show business, so is the parent - it is inevitable! I try to educate the parents about the time commitment they will have to invest in their child's career, as well as how to help their child with their auditions. If I could give one piece of advice to parents of young actors, I would recommend not putting excessive emphasis on audition preparation. When children go up for a part, it is imperative to make sure that they understand the circumstances in the scene and the character they are going to play. Practice reading the scene with them, making sure to take breaks frequently. If drilled on the scene too often, the child may take on a monotone, stagnant quality in the read. The goal is to make the scene seem as much like a real conversation as possible.

Michelle Dahlin's Theatrical Workshop for Young Actors has helped many youthful students in landing parts. Call her at (310) 395-5366 for information concerning class schedules.

Atlanta Workshop Players Professional Children's Theater Company
Lynn Stalling

Lynn Stalling has been the talent manager with ON SCREEN Artist Management in Atlanta and the founder and artistic director of the Atlanta Workshop Players Professional Children's Theater Company. Her thoughts are pertinent to the adult as well as the child actor.

Cold readings. Arrgghh! The mere mention of those two words can cause blood pressure to rise and adrenalin to surge. It is truly an actor's nightmare to perform the unknown! So what do you do?

Avoid cold readings at all costs! Arrive at the audition early. Get the script and use your time wisely to familiarize yourself with the script and rehearse scene. Discover the character's goals, motivations, subtext, etc.

Expect the unexpected. Auditions are like improvisations. They are

MASTER THE ART OF COLD READING

always different. You may prepare for one role and be asked to read for another. You may be asked to continue the scene beyond the script. You may be asked to paraphrase, etc. Don't let anything throw you. This is your audition. Slow down, take your time, ask questions, ask for a moment to look over the script. They will usually give it to you. If not, simply smile and do your best.

Practice reading anything and everything OUT LOUD. Parents can help young actors by making reading fun. Read with exciting delivery. Take turns reading with your child. Have young actors read with siblings. Read with distinct characters in mind.

Type yourself objectively and develop a repertoire of characters that are logical for you to play. Make a commitment to their attitudes, moods, accents, etc. Once these characters are highly developed, they can be used at an actual audition. One of your characters is bound to resemble a character in an audition script.

Practice on camera at home. Watch your reading and auditioning technique. Put the script on a clipboard to avoid the nervous rattling of paper. Hold the script on the clip-board to avoid covering your face. Keep your head up and glance down only with your eyes when reading. Look up as often as possible, especially on the first and last lines, as well as all important moments (dramatic, comic, etc.). If the copy is several pages, unstaple them and casually drop them on the floor as you read. This is less distracting than flipping pages. Be sure to number the pages before you audition, so you can easily reassemble them if you are asked to read the scene again.

Remember: the casting directors want you to succeed. They are pulling for you! Relax and do something fun before the audition. Remember to breathe!

Lynn Stalling can be reached at (404) 998-8111.

Debra Watson
Teacher
"Kids need lots of information to feel comfortable in their environment. It's cruel to send children on an interview when they have no clue what's expected of them. I put kids on camera and ask

them 101 questions to make them feel at ease when they finally do go out on an interview. I also encourage parents to ask lots of questions prior to the interview to help their kids loosen up."

When working on cold reading technique, Debra Watson teaches her students how to listen. "I ask them to go home, turn off the audio on the television and watch the person reacting to what's being said. What do they think they're being told? Kids often forget to listen. They'll just memorize their sides or keep their eyes on the page without listening. You need to grasp the words, look at your partner and relate to him without thinking of your next line. How that other person delivers his line may affect how you deliver yours. I'm trying to teach them to be in the moment."

She also encourages young readers to read out loud at least 15 minutes a day at home. It's really important, especially for those with learning disabilities. If you chose the right material that's stimulating and easy to read, it'll make a difference, not only for their acting careers but for their self-esteem." *(Reprinted from Creative Child Magazine)*

Whether you are a young actor, teenage actor, or an adult actor make time to read out loud often during the week. For instance, when reading a new play or script read it through the first time to yourself to help you understand the content. Read it aloud again. Practice lifting your eyes off the page. Read it a third time out loud, lifting your eyes off the page more frequently. This practice will help to sharpen your cold reading skills.

Debra is also a private coach and works with all ages. For more information you can contact her at (310) 273-7608 in Los Angeles or (512) 452-7972 in Texas.

Faith Acting Studios
Dierdre Weston, Artistic Director
I always start off by encouraging the students to read out loud every night before they go to bed (bedtime stories), and also in their spare time. I encourage them to read those famous bedtime stories that will allow them to play various different characters with various voices and begin to use their creativity. It is very important to read OUT

MASTER THE ART OF COLD READING

LOUD for it is that voice that they begin to become comfortable with and LIKE WHAT THEY HEAR. It's a never ending process especially when they are young and just learning to read, or even if they have don't feel comfortable reading in front of others. Practice until they like their voice and can be fluent. Also, it is important to do diction work. Tongue twisters, mouth stretches. These are easy to do on the way to the audition in the car...even when the get there. All these things help them to become more confident in themselves. Don't try to memorize when you get the script. Become familiar with the script by reading it and digesting as much as you can about the character. Directors are more impressed by what you can create than whether you memorized a few lines. Pick out your punch words....words that should be emphasized more that others (there's one in every sentence). Try to gather information about the character through what OTHERS say about you.

Ms. Weston and Executive Director, Nanci Nixon, founded Faith Acting Studios for youth from ages 4-19, beginners through professionals. It is a non-profit multi-cultural visionary program which reinforces positive self images for youth by offering both training and practical work in the performing arts by teaching the how, what and why's behind the acting profession. For more information, call 323-295-4996 or email them at FAITHACTT@AOL.COM

CHAPTER 5

CLASSES FOR THE YOUNG ACTOR (partial listing)

The Actor's Workout Studio	818-766-2171
Class Act...The Young Actor's Studio www.youngactorstudio.com	310-281-7545 818-766-9958
Michelle Dahlin	310-395-5366
J. D. Ferrantino/Sonia Darmei Lopes	310-358-5942
Hulls Actor's Studio	310-828-0632
Koaching Kids & Teens w/Tracy Martin	213-240-8771
Alan K. Lohr voiceoverbootcamp@earthlink.net	818-569-5469
Sandi Shore's Standup Comedy **Class for Children**	213-460-2426
Lynn Stalling	404-998-8111
Debra Watson	512-452-7972 310-273-7608
The David Wells/Sally Piper Studio	818-990-0036
Dierdre Weston/Faith Acting Studios	323-295-4996
Weist-Barron-Hill	818-846-5595

MASTER THE ART OF COLD READING

CHAPTER SIX

COLD READING FOR VOICE – OVERS

James R. Alburger
Author: "The Art of Voice Acting"
The A-B-C's of Cold-Reading
Many actors have a difficult time with cold reading for a number of reasons: for some, it's the lack of time to internalize the character's emotion; for others it may be the necessity to create a believable delivery while reading from a script; and for others it may simply be the challenge of dealing with an extremely short time-frame during which all the component parts of a character and performance must be brought together. In voice-over, we deal with cold reading on a daily basis. A voice-actor will typically receive the script a few minutes before being expected to be in front of the microphone delivering a perfect performance – and this isn't for an audition – it's for a paid booking!

So, how does a good voice-actor do it? There are actually several answers to this question, and most of the techniques that follow are pretty easy to do, once you understand them. But, remember that cold reading is nothing like actually performing on stage or on-camera and there may be certain acting techniques that you'll need to unlearn in order to become a good cold reader.

For my voice-over workshops I've created what I call the A-B-C's of voice-over. The list actually covers the entire alphabet, but I'll only cover A-E here. Some of these techniques may sound familiar, but I've adapted them to be more effective with voice-over and cold reading. As you read through your script, keep these elements in mind and quickly make appropriate choices. Once mastered, you can use these to take your cold reading skills to a new level.

A = AUDIENCE: Who is your character speaking to. It is always one person – never a group, although the one person you are speaking to may be part of a group. Define your one-person audience in as much detail as you can in your imagination. Make a mental picture of her.

MASTER THE ART OF COLD READING

Imagine she is standing right in front of you. Talk to her, not at her.

B = BACKSTORY: The back-story for a cold reading is different from a back-story that might apply for a stage or film performance. You don't have time to develop a long history for your character, the scene, or anything else. In a cold reading, you must come up with something quickly that gives your character a reason to speak. Consider the back-story to be a specific event that occurs immediately before the first word you will be speaking. Figure out what that specific event is. Often, the event is something your audience said or did to which your character is responding. Make it real in your imagination by visualizing the scene and what has just happened.

C = CHARACTER: Who are you as the speaker of the words? Many actors think that they are playing the role of the character. For your character to be real, he/she must take on a life separate from the real you. Even though you are bringing your life experience to the performance, you – as the actor – must get out of your own way to allow the character to come through and be real. To do this, create a vivid image of the character in your imagination, with as much detail as possible: height, weight, appearance, hair color, jewelry, etc. The more vivid the image, the more real the character will be. Body language and physical movement of your character are extremely important. Allow the character you've created in your imagination to momentarily take over your body in every way. The character you create must live before and after the words in the script. You'll usually be able to glean enough information about your character from a quick scan of your lines.

D = DESIRES: What are your character's intention, wants and needs? What does your character want from saying those words? For effective cold-reading, you must be able to make valid choices as to what your character wants and needs as you are reading the script, even though you may not have a chance to pre-read. Your character's intention will determine her attitude and physical energy.

E = ENERGY: Bob Bergen, one of many voice-actors who replaced the late, great Mel Blanc, once said "Physicalize the moment and the voice will follow." As you make choices for your Audience, Back-story, Character, and Desires, you will simultaneously be uncovering the physical aspects of the performance. How does your character move?

CHAPTER 6

How loud does she speak? At what speed? What is her attitude? What facial expressions does she use? How does her body move? All of these attributes contribute to the overall energy of the performance. Discover what that energy is and be consistent throughout your cold reading. Occasionally, the energy will change during the course of the script. Be aware of when that happens and allow your character to be real and expressive through both the words and physical energy.

The trick to mastering these techniques and becoming an expert at cold reading is to become so good at them that you don't have to think about what you are doing. Once mastered, you'll be able to take any script, do you're A-B-C's in about 30 seconds or less – and know exactly what is needed without even thinking. When you can do that, you will truly be out of your own way, your characters will be real, and you'll be able to cold read just about any script with a minimum amount of preparation.

For more information, visit Mr. Alburger's website: www.voiceacting.com.

Michael Bell
Actor

Listen to old movies and tape the voices of those wonderful character actors. Play that tape in your car for one week. If it takes 2 weeks, so be it. Unless you have a spot on your lung, you have plenty of time. When that character is yours, move on to another one. If you think you have 100 characters, you need a doctor not an agent. Five realized characters is gold. Ninety-five caricatures is straw.

Study improv and while you develop characters…you might develop a funny bone or even better, meet that special person.

It's not about a great voice…it's about knowing your character from every angle. It's about acting. Pavrotti has a great voice…I don't want to hear him as Wendel the Newt.

When you "voice off", you had better be honest to all facets of that character or you will sound like a sock puppet. (My apologies to all sock puppets reading this book).

Last bit if wisdom. If you take a job away from me as a result of my advice, I will find you and rip out your uvula.

Women In Animation
Vonna Bowen
This Voiceover Workout class meets Monday evenings from 7:30 to 9:30 PM at Take Refuge Studios located at 631 Allen Ave., Glendale, CA. Women In Animation members pay $8 per session and non-members pay $12. The fees cover the cost of our engineer. Beginning workout techniques are not taught in the sessions. The actor goes straight to the mic. However, you may audit the session without going to the mic for free. For more information call 818 508-1950.

Voice-Over Bootcamp
Alan K. Lohr
The most fundamental aspect of voiceover work is the cold reading. A cold reading in voiceovers is when the actor has to read copy that they have not seen or have not had a director coach them on. I have always stressed this ability and it is the first technique that is taught to the newcomer to voiceovers.

Cold readings prepare the V-O actor for the more difficult aspects of reading. In the days before computers at radio stations, disc jockeys and newsmen practiced what is known as "Rip and Read". This was when an important piece of information or news story was "hot off the wire'. The on-air staff had to read the copy without prior knowledge of what the copy contained.

Cold readings also bring about "a stream of consciousness" to the voiceover actor. The ability to THINK about what you are talking about is very important in animation, commercials and narration. It sounds like that person is talking only to one person, not many. One to one. In summary, cold readings are an intricate part of the voiceover actor's repertoire.

National Voice Database
While I was surfing the internet looking for ways for voice-over artists and singers to really break into the voice-over business, I came across

CHAPTER 6

the National Voice Database. On this site you will find resources helpful to both the entry level and the professional voice-over artist and jinglist. In addition to this extensive voice resource center, the National Voice Database offers their members a voice website complete with a photo or logo, a voice resume, voice demo(s) and each member gets their own personal website address.

The National Voice Database is doing extensive marketing research to learn the best ways for the voice-over artist and jinglists to use their individual websites to market their voice in order to get more auditions and work opportunities. After looking at their membership application, I found that the information that they request about your vocal abilities would best be answered by getting feedback while filling out the form. A good cold reading exercise that you could do with your peers or your coach would be to cold read copy in order to help you accurately describe your voice and abilities. The more accurate you are the better for you, and for the buyers of voice talent. I have found that voice-over workshops actually teach in detail how to describe your voice. A great way to begin learning more about your voice! On the voice resource division you will find the voice workout section which gives you ideas on places that you can volunteer your voice in exchange for a good cause and experience.

It looks like this is only the beginning of the soon to be most powerful voice-over website in the industry. On the sample site you will find websites of some of the members including Jonathan Frakes (Star Trek), Dennis Franz (NYPD Blues), Tara Charendoff (Rugrats), Joe Alaskey (Daffy the Duck) and more.

We all know the voice over industry can be a fun, lucrative addition to our careers, whether part-time or full-time. We also know that it is a very hard section of the industry to break into and become established. These days there are any number of household name movie and television stars who have lent their voices, whether recognizable or not, to many areas within the voice-over genre itself, from animation to commercials.

For more information on the National Voice Database, contact Betty at 310-273-WORK or at www.voicedatabase.com.

MASTER THE ART OF COLD READING

Mary Grover, M.A.,
Licensed Voice Therapist, Vocal Coach
Actors and voice-over artists might encounter the following problems:
Coughing, throat clearing, dehydration, hoarseness, nasal congestion, laryngitis, bronchitis, dysphonia, voice problems related to allergies, dry scratchy throat, throat irritation, sinus problems, colds and flu, asthma, stuffy head, mucus/phlegm on vocal cords.

For voice talent I recommend the following vocal hygiene tips: avoid coughing, throat clearing and dehydration. Drink at least a half-gallon of water per day. Avoid caffeine. Avoid eating close to bedtime to avoid reflux (stomach acids regurgitated back up esophagus end burning the vocal cords during sleep). When the area around the vocal cords is burned by stomach acid, there is a sphincter like action of the muscles that tightens the throat and squeezes the cords and causes vocal damage. To facilitate alleviation of the above problems I recommend using steam inhalation in conjunction with my vocal hygiene tips listed above.

Ms. Grover has taught voice-over 25 years in the US and around the world, known as a voice "Miracle Worker". Clients include Academy Award and Grammy Award winners as well as jazz, pop, rock, country, R&B, Broadway and classical performers. Her clientele also includes numerous film and sit-com actors.

Call the Voice Care Hot Line 1-800-787-7731 for further tips and advice regarding vocal problems and information on voice care or send email to marygrover@aol.com. For more information, call Ms. Grover at (818) 787-7664 or fax to (818) 780-0698.

The Famous Radio Ranch
Dick Orkin
I called a plumber to my house the other day. My hot water tank was leaking. He walked into the house with his tools, announced he was a plumber and began checking the pipes beneath the kitchen sink. I told him the problem was the hot water heater outside the house. He then banged on some pipes under the house and left, believing his work done. It wasn't. My hot water heater was still leaking.

CHAPTER 6

What's wrong with this incident? Must I tell you? The dumb plumber had absolutely no idea what he was doing. He didn't hear the dispatcher or me tell him that our problem was a leaking hot water heater. In other words, he didn't listen or get the back-story necessary to do his work properly.

This is precisely how many radio voice-over people stand before a microphone and read the text. It's also why they have so many problems with cold readings. They're just banging around, hoping their self-designation (voice-over person) and their tools of vocal tricks and shticks, along with the accumulated baggage of past performances, will handle the job. It won't. And in a cold reading competition, they'll be doing the banal "voice-focused" reads of every other actor. They haven't read the text for story content, which is not just the words on the page, but the story that took place moments or hours or days before the printed copy begins. It's also found in the ideas beneath and between the words. All copy has a back-story potential-single voice or dialogue—if the performer is using their important all-purpose tool, their imagination.

Even if a piece of copy routinely begins, "Right now, the Ace Hardware stores are having a sale on light bulbs," the back-story could be that a friend (always visualize someone you know or knew) tells you he or she is always bumping into the furniture and falling down because the house is too dark. You then suggest he or she needs some more lamps and light bulbs and their reply is that bulbs are expensive. So your first line of the copy, filled with the emotional tone of a previously experienced moment (here's an opportunity, klutz!), then becomes a reply to what precedes the opening line of the text.

This is one of hundreds of back stories that could be used for this copy and if you find my story a lame one, then come up with a better one, but do it fast in a first reading. You say you're not good at this kind of thing. Then practice it. And remember that you're never just talking to the microphone and an invisible audience. It's always another person who is the mike or on the other side of it. And it's someone you know. Their presence is so palpable, you can smell their scent, see their eyes, feel their energy.

The constant exercise of talking "to " a real someone and not "at" an invisible someone and then finding the conversation that comes right

MASTER THE ART OF COLD READING

before the first line of single voice copy or the emotional conflict situation in a dialogue text, leads to the mastery of easily and quickly finding a back story. These new habits become the radio performers best friend in auditions. Without them, you're just banging away at the kitchen sink when you should be working on the hot water heater.

Voice Box Studios
Deborah Sale

As a voice-actor, cold reading skills have an immediate and direct impact on your ability to work. Often, with voice-over work, the term "cold reading" should be changed to "ice-cold reading." Normally an actor only needs to master the art of fast choices and smooth reading for an audition, but imagine showing up for an industrial or recorded book session and being handed thirty or forty pages of material you've never seen before. You will not have time to carefully dissect this new text. You'll have to make quick, active choices on the fly.

There is one, invaluable exercise that I assign to all of my voice-over students – to read aloud from a magazine, book or newspaper for ten to twenty minutes a day. Seems simple enough. After all, you've probably been reading aloud since the second grade. Unfortunately most people have been reciting, not reading. Reading aloud requires the same active choices as performing a play.

Do not pre-read the text. Instead, quickly scan to get the gist of style and content. Decide who you are as the reader/storyteller. Is this a story that happened to you or are you simply sharing information? How close are you going to be, emotionally, to the subject matter? Then, most importantly, decide to whom you are telling the story. Make it a real person - someone that you know. See them sitting in front of you waiting to hear what happens next. Look up from time to time to get their reaction and make sure they're following you. Tape yourself doing this. It may take some time to keep your audience in mind, keep the pace lively, easy to listen to and maintain your character, but with practice, it's a skill well worth developing.

Deborah Sale is a professional voice-actor who also teaches commercial and animation voice-over privately. Call her at 1-800-301-8666 plus the access code 87 or 800-301-TOON+UP. For classes and more information about Voice Box Studios, call Bob Wood at 310-659-3260.

Cold Reading for Voice-Overs

CHAPTER 6

ADR Voice Services
Burt Sharp
In having cast at least 600 features films and television projects as well as animation and commercial voice-overs, this is an observation I'd like to pass on to actors who audition for voice-over roles. When you are given "sides" or copy for the audition, you must make a strong, solid choice on how you will perform the text. Weak, tentative, timid, undecided approaches will not work. You go into the audition as a committed actor who can make a choice, right or wrong. You will gain the respect of the people running the audition who will be more likely to give you a direction to read than just dismissing you as a dull, uninteresting, uncommitted actor.

Besides talent, you need courage to be a great voice-over actor. Showing your ability to make choices demonstrates you are a prepared, thinking actor and not someone waiting to be told what to do. Go get 'em.

Marjory Taylor, Phd., Ed.D.
Voice Mastery
To master the art of cold reading one must have a "sound production machine" that will handle any character or interpretation that comes to mind when you pick up the script. Most actors have a very limited range of pitches and dynamics that can be recorded. If the sound level is low, the resonance disappears, and if the part calls for strong delivery, the voice just gets uglier as it gets louder.

The creation of a professional "sound production machine", as experienced in VOICE MASTERY, allows you to produce a very wide range of controllable, usable pitches, virtually the entire piano keyboard, and do it comfortably on the twenty-third take of a squeaky mouse if necessary.

When the placement or focus of the voice is right, the range of dynamics (loudness) is more than could possibly be needed in recording and the sound maintains its pleasing resonance. The attitudes or emotions that are called for by the script call for various 'colors' of the voice which can be achieved by the adjustment of the width and length of the resonance cavities. The human voice is unique in its ability to direct and shape its resonance. Modulation (the ability to change pitches within the word) is essential for a sensitive interpretation. I call that 'micro-modulation'. The ability to change pitches to express great changes of emotion, or the voice of an entirely different character, I call 'macro-modulation'. There are thirty-two researched emotions and thirty-six 'awareness levels'. It improves your choices and diagnostic ability tremendously if you are familiar with these. The potential for character delineation can include such aberrated speech as stammering, stuttering, lisping, tremolos, nasality, raspiness, or even the one-tone vibration of a robot. These skills are easily accomplished with mastery of the soft palate muscles.

People who come to me often think that when microphones are used, as in all cold reading, film, and radio work, that breath support is not a significant factor. Would it surprise you to learn that unless the consonants are produced by a diaphragm stretched like the head of a drum (your speaker) they simply cannot be consistently clear no matter how many tongue twisters and lip projection exercises you have done. This does not include the necessity for the clarity of the vowels. If you want a "Mickey Mouse" or "Donald Duck" career, STAMINA is still essential to maintain vocal clarity and excellent diction - in other words to stay in character. Very high speed readings can be produced clearly if they are done off a tightly stretched diaphragm. A prime consideration in all professional vocal work is the health and longevity of your instrument. Without a strong "hook-up" to the lowest part of the body, sound quality and a long career simply can't be guaranteed. Knowledge, skill and confidence equal speed. The speed at which one can pick up a script and perform it correctly is crucial. You are exceptionally lucky when the material is good for you. Luck doesn't have to enter in when YOU are good for the material.

For more information, contact Ms. Taylor at 310-246-1743.

Rick Zeiff's Unbelievably Fun Over Class
Rick Zeiff
Rick has been teaching voice-over in Los Angeles for many years. He has ongoing classes and produces and directs voice-over demos. He also casts voice-over animation, including the Oscar-winning animated short "The ChubbChubbs," as well as industrials, books on

tape, etc... Moreover he casts and is directing "Gundam Force," an animated series for "The Cartoon Network."

There is no auditing, but Rick will explain in length his philosophy and how he works and is happy to answer any questions. There is no need to audition but feel free to call us at 323-651-1666 if you would like more information.

VOICE-OVER LISTINGS (partial listing)

Wally Burr Recording	818-845-0500
Louise Chamis	818-985-0130
Aliso Creek Voice Over Workshops	818-954-9931
Bill Dearth, The Speech Mechanic	818-761-1051
Dishu Arts Connection Accent Reduction Class	818-755-0049
Freedom of Speech	323-668-9812
Robert Easton/The Henry Higgins of Hollywood	818-985-2222
Mary Grover, M.A.	800-787-7731
Voiceover Boot Camp	818-569-5469
Original Voice Bank	818-846-2002
The Famous Radio Ranch	323-462-4966
Professionally Speaking With Julie Daniels	818-623-8960
Sound Concepts, Inc. www.soundconceptsinc.com	800-451-8560
Marjory Taylor PHD., ED.D	310-246-1743
Voice Box Studios	310-854-6788

MASTER THE ART OF COLD READING

The Voice Over Connection, Inc. 213-384-9251
www.voconnection.com

Voice Overs One on One With Ellen Yuen 818-766-1866

Rick Zeiff's Unbelievably Fun Voice Over Class 323-651-1666

CHAPTER SEVEN
CHICKEN SOUP FOR YOUR CAREER

The following section contains a little bit of everything for everybody! These highly regarded industry professionals have put pen to paper (most likely fingers to keyboard) to share their wisdom and collective years of insight concerning some of the different areas that actors deal with in their ever expanding careers.

Warm Up a Cold Reading With Improv
(WHAT DO YOU MEAN, MAKE IT UP?)
Pat Dade

Ten years ago I walked into an audition I had read about in the newspaper. The ad heralded the creation of a new comedy group that relied solely on improvisation. I was skeptical but also curious, and because no preparation was required, I just decided to check it out. The audition consisted of being run through a series of "theatre games", tried and true methods designed to heighten the actor's awareness of character and environment while in the rehearsal phase of production. They actually expected me to make it up and trust that whatever came out of my mouth and whatever I did physically was okay. They told me there's no failure in improv, only failure to follow through. It was the coolest audition I ever had. Ten years later and I still perform with and teach for that national improvisational troupe in Los Angeles — ComedySportz.

One thing I had not banked on at the time was that improv would do much more than give me a performance outlet and a chance to cut up on-stage and actually have people pay to watch us do it. I walked into an audition for a musical and found that the accompanist was held up in terrible traffic and could not even imagine that he would make it. To make a long story short, we were asked to improvise a song, just so they could hear our voices and see how we handled ourselves on stage. Forget the prepared song, just make it up. I could see beads of sweat breaking out on the foreheads of my fellow actors. I, however, relished the opportunity to perform without the proverbial net. It was a great audition and, yes, I got the part.

MASTER THE ART OF COLD READING

How does it work?
We're trained as actors to rely on a set of tools that when used properly, will never fail us. But what happens when conditions change, the unexpected happens and things go awry? What happens when rogue actors decide to shake things up or memory fails us at inappropriate moments? The onus is on you to make it happen. Improv training can improve your chances of getting through moments like these. And not just getting through, but succeeding.

You are taught to think differently, to see your environment, the objects and the people in it on new levels. You learn how to work with the empty space and spark the imagination of those who would normally watch passively, to take part and invest in what you do. Improv training allows you to work without the luxury of time to think. You simply do. You learn to make quick decisions and act immediately. Most importantly, you learn to trust yourself.

Start with an improv class and you'll start taking risks you normally would never take. If you never volunteer to do be the first to do things now, expect that to change. With confidence comes the desire to try things that have never been tried — you'll want to see things with fresh new eyes.

Cold readings will not make your blood run cold. Your training and trust will give you the confidence you need to make a decision and stick with it. And when the director or auditors offer an adjustment, you won't think "I guess I did it wrong the first time," but "Wow, I get to do it a whole new way this time." My rule of thumb has always been that auditors don't know what they're looking for until you show it to them. With improv skills under your belt, you'll have so much more to show. You'll have a Rolodex in your head and every card will be totally accessible at a moment's notice, and you'll trust your choices.

How do I get started?
There are several improv groups in the Los Angeles area to consider: The Groundlings, ComedySportz, Improv Olympics, Theatre Sports to name only a few (my apologies to those I didn't mention!). Check the trades and free presses for ads about classes and workshops. Call them up and audit so you can participate in the class rather than sit in the back and watch. Improv only works by doing. The sooner you

break down the "I can't" barrier, the better you will feel and the easier it will become to think on your feet. And remember, you may not be "stage - ready" after your first five or six classes, but you will notice a major attitude adjustment when you hit your next audition. Like all acting techniques, it takes constant study to keep sharp and fresh (I've been performing improvisation for over ten years, yet I still meet once a week with company to practice!)

If you would like to read more about improvisation, start by picking up a copy of Viola Spolin's "Improvisation For The Theatre" or "Improv" by Kenneth Johnstone. If you're at a loss for what to do after that, just make it up!

The Truth - It'll Getcha Every Time
Sam Christensen, Career Consultant/Coach
"Tell me a little about yourself?" That's one of the roughest requests that you face on a regular basis. What do I say? Do I recite my resume? Do I recount some amusing experience on the way to the appointment? Do I flatter the casting director? ("Gee, that's a beautiful tie!") Actually, all of these are great conversational ploys. However, what's supposed to be accomplished in the three, four, or five minutes that you're given is to create some memorability. After the three months passes between the time of this short interview and the moment a role you're right for is actually being cast, will you be remembered and make the audition list? So, "Tell me a little about yourself" translates to, "Tell me something by which I'll be able to remember who you are."

Now, I don't know about you, but in an interview situation, it's always the lie that comes back and bites me on the butt. If I've fibbed a little and usually for me that's about being late or not returning a phone call I fully intended to - it's always the little fib I can't quite remember. There I am, the teeth-marks of a lie smarting my posterior. But when I stick to the truth and say, "Sorry I was late - it's a bad habit," or, "Pardon me, I neglected to call you back," then it's easy. Because you don't have to figure out which little white lie you told. It's no problem. You can always remember the truth. That's the power of it.

You can be memorable in a very short amount of time. You can let people know as much as possible about yourself. You can be genuine and interesting. What's easy to remember? What rings true? - THE TRUTH! Just because it's true, it works.

That's what the Sam Christensen Process is all about: arming you with ways to tell the truth about yourself so that you can be fully appreciated and always remembered. The work you did helped you know what others are thinking, integrate that awareness with your own perception and, thus, arrive at identity - what everybody knows about you.

The essences you chose and the conversational vocabulary that you created give you a myriad of preferred ways to say: Here's who I am. I know you've already noticed. When I mention the truth I recognize about myself and you've already observed it, you know I'm onto it and I'm able to use my own "stuff" to make the characters I create unique and personal.

Marketing is about making the truth eminently available to people. The window you have may be brief - a glance at a picture or a cover letter, a short interview - the brevity of your opportunity is another reason the truth is crucial. If they're only giving you a glance, or thirty seconds to tell your life story, you'd better fill that time with something potent and unforgettable. Truth has power beyond what you can imagine until you put it into practice.

For more information, visit Mr. Christensen's website:
www.samchristensen.com

The Importance of Cold Reading Classes
Cherie Franklin
When actors come to Los Angeles to find work, they soon realize that auditions are a split second long. They walk in and a cold reading is asked of them. Not much time to prepare and you get one shot to nail the reading. Theatrical and film training may not prepare you for the cold reading experience. The new actor discovers that Los Angeles is a cold reading town. One second you're in and a few minutes later, you're out. How do actors begin to prepare for a cold reading? They learn the mechanics of a cold reading before they walk into the audition.

CHAPTER 7

It is the mistaken belief of many actors that a cold reading is a hit or miss circumstance. The copy is read over once or twice and they've either got it or they don't. When they consistently don't get the callback, they finally realize that they are lacking somewhere. They have already spent the big bucks on intensive workshops without ever finding out exactly how to make the cold reading work for them. So, despite as much training as they have had in acting, they now enter the cold reading system.

As in every endeavor in life, you should take one step at a time to find out the one thing that works best for you, and continue on in that positive direction. First, the actor needs to find out exactly what a cold reading is. One class can tell you that. The next class you take should channel your direction to get that cold reading up to par and portray exactly what you want to do every time you read before a casting director.

One description of a cold reading could go something like this:
You are given the copy, which, in your opinion, has an inadequate amount of information. You've got less than thirty minutes to bring it to life. You read opposite someone who gives you nothing to work off of, all the while trying to remain calm, confident and brilliant. Actors can get discouraged if they have no idea of how to tackle any one of these obstacles, especially in that short amount of time. Unfortunately, that is exactly what is expected of you.

Your first cold reading workshop will provide you with a good introduction. Your second, third and fourth classes should be giving you the game plan that you required to nail each and every cold reading. You need a realistic and practical technique that will help you to produce the best cold reading that you can. In this split-second town, it is essential that you possess a technique that can make you a success in any situation, one that produces positive results on the spot, unlike one that requires you to study with Tibetan monks for five years before you are ready. Nor do you need any one workshop that encourages you to remain in their system to keep your confidence alive. Workshops should give you tools and techniques that you require and then set you free.

Preparation is the Key
You know your call time is 1:00. Show up at noon. If you get a call

MASTER THE ART OF COLD READING

that only allows you thirty minutes or less to get the side and prepare, utilize every second of that time in preparation. There is no time to socialize. You are on a job interview. That job has just been handed to you in script form. You must adapt immediately, not only to the role, but to your surroundings. Preparation and practice makes perfect! A good, strong cold reading class should teach you how to break down a side completely and do it in a short amount of time. All the specifics to perform the part are in the sides. Most actors and actresses know that they can do the role once they get the job. Unfortunately, you must do the role now and you've got five minutes to prove it. The short amount of time you are allowed does not minimize the skills required. It demands that you be specific, strong and focused.

A cold reading class should keep you prepared. The ultimate responsibility of being a creative, capable and professional actor lies with you. Comprehensive study is involved in any job in which you choose to be a professional. Find the class that gives the ability to prepare a complete, strong, and accurate cold reading in thirty minutes or less. The callbacks will come if you are prepared.

Cold Reading for Commercials
Megan Foley

Every commercial read is a cold read. The current cold reading workshops will not help you with your commercial auditions. What you need is a good on-camera commercial class. If you have a home video camera, tape yourself reading from commercial copy in a magazine.

I was trained for the stage, but when I switched to commercials I had a very hard time. I had difficulty with developing a character so quickly, and working with cue cards, I also had to learn to be more intimate, and less theatrical.

Bad cue card reading takes place when an actor's eye is locked on the cure-card and never connects with the camera. Commercials are more natural now than they were in the 70's. Then, the actor always looked directly to the camera. Today they are like little films.

As far as dressing for a commercial audition. You should never go as far as going out and renting a costume. That's too much. Example: If you are coming in for a military role, wear a Khaki shirt; if you're coming in for a bride, don't fully dress up, just pull your hair up and perhaps put a flower there, it's that simple. What sells an actor, other than his face and look is his confidence and not being needy. So, relax, come in with self-conveyance, show the casting director how good you are and then leave.

The most important thing I can tell an actor who is auditioning for a commercial is to know and understand the copy and to listen. The biggest complaint directors have is that the actor "doesn't get it" or that he "doesn't listen to direction." Be prepared and relaxed so you can be ready for direction. Be prepared and relaxed so you can be ready to audition. Bring something to the party - don't walk in and say "I can be anything you want." Walk in and say "This is what I can give to you." Bring your creative energy and drive to every single audition. Also, be prepared to get no direction and listen and adjust if you do get direction. Be flexible and ready for anything. Don't give a generic audition. Commit to choices that are unique for you and go all the way with them. Strong choices are made when you ask the questions. How do I feel? Do I like the product that is being advertised? Are you happy to be there?

It is important to have a good slate. (That's announcing your name into the camera.) Slate with the essence of your character. It works every time. If you don't have one or it is an interview audition, have a nice warm, friendly slate or one that shows your personality. Above all, enjoy your auditions. Treat our career as a business - give it as much attention as you would any other career (or your day job!). It will never truly be your career until you give it your all constantly. Love it and enjoy it. If you find yourself resenting auditions take a break and come back when you are refreshed and enthusiastic.

An Acting Seminar With...
Raymond Forchion, EEOC Chairman, Actor, Teacher
The ability to cold read is a major necessity in this business. It still seems to be the best way for an actor to be seen in consideration for a particular role. Though what is interesting, is that once you reach a certain level within your body of work, the "star" level, the need to be read decreases. Many times you begin to be hired on the basis of your past work. But

MASTER THE ART OF COLD READING

sooner or later there comes that role that even the best known actors of our business find themselves having to read for. Perhaps it is in a genre the actor is not known for, comedy instead of drama, for instance. At that point the same skills are needed in terms of the read.

One of the great mistakes many novice actors make is to not also have a solid background of training. The ability to cold read is only one of your tools. I always stress the fact that good cold reading technique is very important, but you must back it up with the skills of a well-trained actor. Know how to analyze the material and make the most exciting right choices for the role. We can debate the skills of many of the most successful actors in our business and how they got there, but usually you can't deny the excitement that they create in the audience that sustains them. We all have different paths. It is our job to find the path that best leads us to an exciting, real and moving performance.

We must always remember our audience and what we want to communicate. Many actors, because of our love for what we do, and the emotional stimulation of our work, forget that we are doing it for an audience. ACTING WITHOUT AN AUDIENCE IS THERAPY. If your work doesn't move that audience, or casting person, then you may have failed in the task you set out to do when you audition, which is to show the casting director who you are as an artist. I like to think that we are never auditioning for one role, but hopefully for everything that casting director will ever cast. As an actor, you never want to be cast in the wrong role. That happens all the time. One thing that wise directors are often wary of, as are wise casting directors, is the actor who is a great cold reader, but never rises or moves beyond that in the actual performance. Sometimes you can be fooled. Good cold reading technique is not a substitute for good acting technique, it should be in addition to good acting technique.

One thing that I have seen repeatedly, watching thousands of actors as Chair of the Screen Actors Guild Casting Committee over the past few years, is a major lack of movement and vocal training. Actors in a very small environment often can't be heard by the casting directors and are constantly upstaging themselves. This is a lack of basic training, one-on-one. Yes, the camera will move in for our close-ups and we will have microphones on the set, but still the basic rules apply. Why so many of the acting teachers out there are not teaching this I don't know, but you want to look professional when you are about to work. Often, when an actor can't be heard, it may be because they don't really feel THEY ARE WORTHY OF BEING HEARD. Lack of confidence kills auditions and performances. Often a confident actor with less skills will get a role over a more skilled actor with less confidence. Good cold reading and acting technique gives the performer more confidence and the casting director more confidence to stake their reputation on you.

Cold Reading for Stand Up Comics
Mark Lonow, Co-Owner of the world famous Improv Comedy Club
Comics should always remember when performing their stand-up act they are also practicing for other performance situations: commercials, sit-coms, movies and "straight plays". The character being developed during the years of stand-up is usable in these other forms, as long as certain rules of acting are adhered to.

First, with acting (i.e. cold reading), unlike with stand-up, the audience must be held at arm's length from the performance. The audience must simply become voyeurs comfortably watching from outside the interplay between the performers on stage. To do this, the actor must create what is called the "fourth wall" or imaginary wall between themselves and the audience. This is accomplished by mentally picturing things that might exist on the downstage wall, the wall between the performer and the audience, if that wall were to exist. What the performer does is actually identify easily visible objects in the auditorium (exit light, brass rails, shining banisters, etc.) or auditorium room (pictures of the executive, plaques, posters, etc) and ascribe to these objects the identity of household objects (paintings, lamps, tables, etc.) which might exist in the room that the scene is taking place in. Then, whenever the performer's eyes wander downstage and out to the audience (casting director, producer, etc.) they can fix their gaze on that which was previously plotted out and imagine they are simply looking at an extension of the imaginary room they created from the scene. This also helps allow the actor to feel comfortable with certain feelings that otherwise might not be comfortable in public.

The second difference between stand-up and acting is that unlike stand-up, in acting, a character grows and changes. When people in

MASTER THE ART OF COLD READING

a scene say something, the words spoken should affect every other person in the scene. Therefore the character that was created for the stand-up must listen and allow the dialogue said by others to affect his or her responses and doing so color the words that are said in reply. With this being true, in a cold reading, the performer must allow for any unplanned emotional responses to enter the scene that he or she might have.

Actors in scenes, and especially cold reading scenes, should always be working. When they are not talking it does not mean that they are not present: thinking and feeling. The performer should always be conscious of how what is being said is effecting their lives and emotions. These emotions must be allowed to play out not only within the actor's body but also on the actor's face. That does not mean the emotions are not exaggerated or "cartooned" but are given a chance to exit through the eyes and face.

Lastly, under the pressure of a cold reading, that actor who has been trained in stand-up usually goes for a big, all encompassing performance. Most often that bigness is incorrect. Remember, small and intimate is best for the movie or TV camera and for most cold readings. Small and intimate also gives the performer greater control of delicate emotions that might be called for in an acting performance and not called for in his or her stand-up.

There are so many variables to take into account when performing in a cold reading that it is impossible to list them all in a few paragraphs, but if the above mentioned rules are followed, they will go a long way towards permitting the stand-up to execute an acting assignment with a good measure of professionalism.

A Casting Director's Perspective
Keith Wolfe, Casting Director/Career Consultant
Cold reading is the method by which casting directors can see many actors in a short period of time. Most projects have many roles that must be cast within a limited amount of time. A casting director may have to see a hundred or more actors for a single role before finding exactly what the producer and director are looking for.

While casting a movie, I once interviewed over 600 actresses for the lead role. Each actor came in and did a reading for me. I chose the ones who I felt did the best reading and brought them in on call-backs to present to the producer and director.

Did All Actors Do a Cold Reading?
All of the actors who read for my project did a reading, but some auditions were not a cold reading in the purest sense. By that, I mean some of the actors' agents and managers got the material for their clients in advance of the audition date and so those actors were able to prepare for the audition. Other actors showed up for their audition without having seen the material and had only a brief time to prepare. The actors who were able to get the material in advance were much more prepared and, in almost all cases, were able to present themselves and their talent with more confidence and in a more professional manner.

Most of the actors who came without preparation made excuses. Some of the excuses were legitimate — such as they had been out of town, their pager wasn't working, they just heard from their agent, they didn't have transportation to get the sides (pages of script). Regardless of how valid the reason for not having the material in advance, you are certainly at a disadvantage and it makes it hard for you to compete with those who come to the audition prepared. This brings us to the question:

What is a Cold Reading?
Most auditions are referred to as cold readings, but a true cold reading is when you have only a short amount of time to read over your sides before the audition. There are different levels of cold reading according to how much time you have with the material to prepare for your reading. If you have the script or sides for several days and you are able to work on the material with your acting coach, it may appear to the producer and director or casting director that you are doing a great cold reading and that's the impression you want to make. If you had the material for only a few minutes, you may not be able to give your best performance.

For years I have been asked by my consultant clients if they should memorize their scene when going in for the first reading. I turned to one of my friends who was a casting director at Universal for 20 years and asked him the same question. His feeling was the actors should memorize the scene word for word, but hold the script in their hand and look at it from time to time during the reading so as not to give the impression it was memorized and to make sure that if they went up on their lines they could refer to the scene and it would not break their concentration.

Another reason for not making it look like you have the scene memorized is you don't want the director to think this is the best performance you can give. I like my editor Gordon Gale's description of what confronts you with a pure cold reading. In his article "The Art of Cold Reading" he states the following:

"Cold reading is the method used to judge actors who are competing for parts. At an audition, you are given 5 to 15 minutes with a script and no explanation of what happens before or after, who the character is or any textural details. You then go into a room with one to four strangers judging you and probably a camera recording you. You do the script with all the emotional values of a fully rehearsed, blocked and memorized performance, but you are reading and probably working with a scene partner you have never met and have had no chance to confer with. But if you can look good with these obstacles, no one worries about what you'll do on the set. And it can be done."

I agree with Gordon that this type of cold reading is unfair, but it's what you will sometimes face in your pursuit of an acting career.

A Cold, Cold Reading

When I was working as a personal manager, one of my clients was at my office while I was having a conversation with a producer about his casting needs. It turned out that my actor was in the range of the character they were trying to cast. I arranged for my client to leave my office and go straight to see the producer. The actor was not expecting to do a reading when he arrived. He thought it was just a preliminary meeting and he was hoping he could get the script and read it over and prepare for a reading.

When he arrived at the producer's office, he was cordially greeted by the producer and had a great meeting. When he asked if it would be possible to see some of the script, the producer said he was sorry but he didn't have one available. Then the producer turned and began typing and quickly pulled a page out of the typewriter and said,

CHAPTER 7

"Here read this." The actor was relatively new and nearly had a coronary when the producer put him on the spot. This was certainly not fair, but the producer was not trying to trick him. He liked the actor and was trying to provide my client something to audition with.

Producers and directors need talent to make their projects. You may be an excellent actor and just what they are looking for, but if you are not able to make a good impression with your reading, it could keep you from getting a chance to meet them in the call-backs.

I always try to make my casting materials available, as I'm sure other casting directors do. But from time to time, as hard as I try, it just doesn't work out that way. Recently, I was casting a spokesperson for a commercial. I had requested the material in advance but it was not completed. The producer brought it with him to the casting session. He showed up at 10:55 am and the casting session started at 11 am. It was an even playing field because no one had the material in advance.

So when no one has the material in advance who had the advantage at this audition? The actors with the best cold reading skills will, in these types of situations, certainly have a better chance at getting the job.

Does The Best Actor Always Get The Job?
Probably not. For several different reasons. What makes this crazy, but wonderful business so frustrating for new and advanced actors is that you never really know why you didn't get the job. There are many reasons for landing or not landing a role. While your cold reading is extremely important, it is not always the reason you aren't chosen for the role. You may be too tall, too short, too heavy, too skinny, etc. You may also be exactly what they are looking for, but if your cold reading is not up to par, the producer may feel you are not up to doing the role.

Cold Reading — The Key to Call-Backs
There are many things in your career as an actor you cannot control. Did your agent submit your photo for the proper role? Did you have enough time to get to the casting session on schedule? Did the casting director like your photo enough to call you in? Are you the right height or weight? Do you have the right color hair and eyes?

MASTER THE ART OF COLD READING

However, there is one area of your acting career where you have complete control. Training! You can be as good as you want to be as a result of your persistence, determination and desire. Some actors seem to be born with the gift, but for 99.9% of the others, it's hard work, concentration, focus and a good acting coach. You may have to try several acting teachers before you find the right one. Most successful actors credit one or more of their acting coaches for the success they have attained.

There are always exceptions to every rule. And there have been those successful actors who, themselves, have said they had trouble with the auditioning process. Charles Grodin said he was terrible at auditioning which prompted his book, "It Would Be So Nice If You Weren't Here." Sylvester Stallone said he would have never made it if he had to depend on auditioning for roles. A casting director at Universal Studios told me that he had Harrison Ford in for a reading and Harrison did not do very well at cold reading. He was amazed at how, on film, Harrison jumps off the screen at you, but did so poorly with his one-on-one reading.

The Audition is the Job
Cold reading is the audition and the audition is the job. Regardless of how long or how short a time you have the material, for me, it's all about how you do the reading. Some actors have come to my office for a reading after having the material for days, but they didn't get the part.

A good cold reading does not always guarantee you the role, but a bad cold reading almost always guarantees you will not get the role.

Don't let the phrase, "cold reading," lull you into thinking all you have to do is stand there and read. What casting directors, producers and directors are really looking for is someone to walk in and give a great performance. It would be fairer if instead of calling it a cold reading, we called it a mini-performance — since that is the expectation. Make sure your cold reading is the best performance you can give.

The director is looking for someone who can spark his imagination and cold reading is where you will get the chance to win a role that could get your career off and running.

CHAPTER 7

Take charge of your career by making sure your cold reading skills and your acting skills are sharp and ready for any audition that comes your way. If you have made the choice to be an actor, don't just be a good actor. Be a wonderful actor. From time to time an agent will call me and tell me he has a wonderful actor and I should see his client because of how great he is.

Make sure your agent can call me and other casting directors and truly mean it when he tells us how great you are. This is how careers are made. It is up to you to be so good at cold readings that even if you don't get the role you went in to read for, the casting director will tell your agent what a wonderful job you did and will keep you in mind for something else.

Take Charge of Your Career
Only the strong survive in cold readings, prepared auditions and the casting process. Don't be timid or shy when you walk in the door of a casting office. Don't let them see the paper shaking in your hand. You can be as nervous and you need to be, but don't let them see you sweat. When I'm casting a film or commercial I want someone who has confidence in themselves and so does the producer and director. Remember, the casting director, the producer and the director all want you to succeed — they are looking for someone who can do the job.

Don't wait for Hollywood to come knocking on your door. Fuel your imagination with desire and create your future! Take charge of the moment! Take charge of your career by being strong and unshakable when you go in for your next cold reading. God Bless.

Keith Wolfe is an active casting director and career consultant. When time allows he offers free consultations. He is located at the Sunset-Gower Studios in Hollywood. (323) 469-5595. We would like to thank Keith Wolfe and Sliver Screen Publishing for permission to print excerpts from Cold Reading/A Casting Director's Perspective. Other recommended reading by Keith Wolfe: The Right Agent — The Casting Directors — Personal Managers — How To Get Your SAG Card — The Right Photographer.

MASTER THE ART OF COLD READING

My Advice on Cold Reading
Tracy Roberts

I would like to illustrate what I think a great- cold reading should be. I was directing a four-camera show for Warner Brothers/Columbia TV, which my sister and her husband were writer/producers on. We were auditioning actresses for the young female lead. All of the agencies from both coasts, big and small, had submitted clients. Many were pretty, talented and gave good intelligent readings, but no one impressed us enough to test them. One day a girl came in - she hadn't been given the script ahead of time. She took about twenty minutes in the outer office, then said she was ready. As she began to read, my sister nudged me and said sotto voce, "She's not reading the lines!" (Writers are usually very possessive about what they've written). I shushed her and we witnessed a stunning reading. After the actress had left, I assured sister that every line was read as written - no "handles" and no added or subtracted lines, however the behavior was so improvisational that my sister didn't recognize the very scene she had written. The girl, of course, after continuing her fascinating and fresh behavior on subsequent callbacks, got the part. In analyzing what she did, she cold read the way I teach, the way I believe all actors should work on cold readings. She made the lines, attitudes and relationships all her own; her choices were inventive and assured, even in that short time, she took the luxury to discover, to explore. We saw and heard the "music between the notes." We saw and heard the spontaneity - and that's the best way I can sum it up.

Cold reading, is a mandatory technique that the actor must master in order to compete in today's fast paced television and film auditioning process, and ultimately get the part. I've watched actors whom I know are quite, wonderful, give bad cold readings. Most actors deliver cold readings that are intelligent and truthful, but not exciting or fresh or inventive. These are valuable qualities to have and they can be incorporated into the actor's cold reading if the actor learns how to make a marriage with the character. The actor must know what he/she wants, make personal choices in collaboration with the script and then leave him/herself open to react to the moment and their partners. This is especially important if the actor has a partner who gives little or nothing, forcing the actor to intensify his/her own reality.

CHAPTER 7

Casting directors may vary on the types of cold readings they want. Some like "full out" performances, some like low key readings. The actor must know the casting directors preferences, then give a personal, confident, un-cliché cold reading.

Here at our studio, our teachers have different approaches to cold readings because it's important for the actor to be exposed to a variety of cold reading techniques, and we offer a comprehensive program with other classes.

I feel acting is acting and the creative process is the same whether it's for TV, film, the stage, or cold reading. We simply have to adjust our energy to the medium we're working in. scene study work, for me, is a must as is the sensory work so that each actor develops a repertoire of emotional tools that is indigenous to him or herself.

TRACY ROBERTS passed away in February 2002. Her words of wisdom still ring true today. ALUMNI include Laura Dern, Sharon Stone, Heather Locklear, DavidHasselhoff, Jay Leno, Season Hubley, George Wendt, Nia Peoples, Doug Savant, Jason Brooks and many more.

How to Have Your "Best Shot" at Cold Readings and Auditions
Alisha Tamburri, Photographer
A headshot is an actor's calling card; your single most important marketing tool whether new or a working actor. And because casting directors and agents are bombarded with hundreds of headshots weekly, your picture must leap across the desk at them. In the words of the casting director, Joey Paul, "The image must speak to me and I, in turn, act on that as a buyer of talent."

Getting the perfect photograph means finding the perfect photographer - one with instinct, patience, and vision. Look for someone with technical wizardry and inside knowledge of how the entertainment industry works. After all, a career can be made in the blink of an eye.

Cold Reading Workshops
It is crucial to bring a photo to all cold reading workshops. An actor's photo is his/her tool for being remembered. The person conducting

the workshop may be interested in hiring you for an upcoming project - you never know when your type is needed. If your cold reading class is a soap workshop, bring a sexy photo. If your workshop focuses on sitcoms, choose a photo with upbeat energy. And a strong, powerful shot is best for a dramatic workshop. Not sure what direction you want your career to go in? Do your homework. Know how others perceive you and how you perceive yourself. The moment you walk into a casting session, you are cast. Actors must know their essences, their qualities, and the first impressions they leave others with.

What is an Effective Photo?
An effective photo should not only have personality, charisma, intensity, and warmth, but sharpness and clarity. It must look like you at your best or your worst, depending if you are a lead actor or a character actor. If what you love to do is comedy, your photos should be full of pizazz. If you are a dramatic actor, your picture should reflect depth and soul. And for those interested in acting for soap operas, strive for a beautiful, alluring shot. No matter what the role, a headshot should always have something going on in the eyes.

How to Find a Photographer
When looking for a photographer, trust recommendations from agents, casting directors, and acting coaches. Referrals from friends who "just love their new photos" are also helpful. An actor must not only like the photographer's work, but like the photographer. A face-to-face meeting offers a chance to get to know one another, evaluate chemistry, and view the photographer's work. The photographer you shoot with should be professional, caring, flexible, and fun. Ask yourself, "Is this someone I am comfortable enough around to let go and be myself?"

A photographer's work is a reflection of their background. How many years has he/she been in the business? Is this person committed to a career in photography, or are they just looking to make some extra money on the side?

A photographer's headshot book should be full of black and white, commercial and theatrical shots. Look for actors of all ages, races, sizes, and types. It is also a real plus when a photographer has a book of proof sheets as well. Proof books, which show an entire session

CHAPTER 7

versus just one good shot, should give a feel for the versatility of a photo shoot.

Proofs are also a way to gauge a photographer's style. Not only should a photographer be in-sync with the industry-end of taking pictures and the latest trends, they should be in-sync with you. The individuality of a client should always over-ride any imposed photography style. A good photographer adapts to whatever qualities the actor brings to a session.

The Importance of the Process
Another area to research is a photographer's process. A good photographer captures what is inside that person. After all, your photos must represent you and be full of looks you can achieve on your own. For any given audition, an actor must walk in looking like his/her headshot. But how does a photographer capture your many sides? I enjoy directing, doing improv, chatting, or having an actor take on a character. I align myself with your interests and we play. To avoid awkward shots of actors placed in stilted positions, avoid photo sessions that are mere posing sessions. A session should be a celebration of energy, creativity, and YOU. How better to capture your personality then to put you in a safe, relaxed, fun environment, dressed in your favorite clothes with your favorite music playing in the background!

After the Shoot
The headshot process is not over when you leave the studio. A professional photographer guides you every step of the way by processing your film, marking the best frames from your proof sheets, cropping your photos, and making sure your finished 8x 10's look fantastic. I will also refer you to a quality reproduction house and retoucher if necessary. You are an actor, not a model, so perfection is not the goal. Retouching should be reserved for blemishes or bags under the eyes, rather than major over-hauls. Please make sure your reproductions are PHOTOS, not lithographs. Remember a headshot can launch a career!

Coloring Your Audition With Jill Kirsch
Angel Harper
Jill Kirsch's clients want to look their best at every audition. She

MASTER THE ART OF COLD READING

believes that individuals can be defined into four rotor groups: Spring, Summer, Winter, or Fall. Jill explains, "Seasonal names are arbitrary ways of referring to color groups. Within each palette you get every color. Some blues have a lot of yellow in them which make them warmer, other blues are very icy." Kirsch maintains the whole mystique of make-up can be lifted if you know what "season" you are.

Let's face it. Your favorite color may not be your best color to wear at an audition, especially an on-camera audition. Kirsch is convinced this simple strategy could have a major impact on helping entertainers look and feel their best. Actors would do better with colors that compliment their skin tone rather than exaggerate it. With too much, "they look painted and false" and with tones that play down their own skin color, "they disappear into the sofa".

Jill Kirsh of The Color Company has been a color consultant for over 15 years. She is a walking advertisement for her successful business. Jill has done numerous celebs ... many that we all know well. When she told me I was "winter', I had no doubt she was right. The truth is everyone can wear every color, it just depends on which shades work best for you. Having your color done by Jill can give you a real edge at your next cold reading workshop or audition. The work matters but it's the whole package they buy.

Robin Lee Knoll, owner of the Casting Break, mentioned that sometimes at commercial auditions, the commercial producer may fast forward through the audition tape with the volume off. When they see an actor that catches their eye, they stop and turn up the volume. In this case, if you have a great audition but you don't stand out visually you might not get called back. When we wear the right color with the right make-up, the right clothes, we come alive in other people's eyes.

Jill will come to your home or office. You then sit in front of a large, lighted mirror and with colorful scarves and swatches you will see for yourself, as I did, which ones dramatically bring out the best in you. The session lasts about 2 hours. For those of you unfamiliar with the approach, here's how it goes: colors are divided into four groups named after the seasons. Earth tones go into the autumn camp, while crisp, clear hues are considered winter, spring colors have a warming, yellow tint, while summer colors have a cooler, blue tone. And, the theory goes, we all have a palette of colors that looks best on us - depending on our hair, tone, and eye color. At the end of the session you will receive a personalized book of fabric swatches that provide the best combinations for you, male or female. Additionally, Jill has developed personalized make-up kits for each seasonal group, as well as classic affordable accessories that include silk scarves and watches.

As a New Yorker, I was skeptical but my vanity and curiosity overcame that. Thanks to Jill's effervescent personality, I enjoyed the labeling process. I was amazed at the difference color made look in terms of age, vitality and charisma. It's a lasting one-time investment and is money well spent not only to look your best, but to aid in future purchases as well. Gift certificates are also available. (818) 760-7798.

Need Help Getting Auditions? Try Personalized Mailings!
Melody Jackson, Smart Girls Productions
Once you have developed a strong audition technique, the next big challenge is getting a chance to use it. Some of the current means for getting auditions are through your agent, casting director workshops, submissions groups, and your own personalized mailings. In this article, I will be focusing on personalized mailings.

When giving advice about anything in the film business, I like to preface it by saying that almost everything has worked at one time or another and nothing works every time. Since starting Smart Girls Productions in 1992, I have continually sought and developed direct mailing techniques to increase your odds for getting calls, in light of whatever limitations you may be facing at a given point in your career. These techniques are used by actors of any age, with or without an agent and credits or union affiliation— although the more you have working in your favor, the better, of course.

First of all, many actors want to know "Do mailings work? Why should I do one? Will it work with my limitations" (whatever they think they are)? Most casting offices, though not all, open every picture that comes across their desks, even if it is only for a fleeting glance at the photo.

So how often should you submit? Casting directors responses vary

MASTER THE ART OF COLD READING

from "anytime you have something going on or some news I should know," to once a month," to "one time only and we keep it on file," to any other variety of answers. My recommendation is to do what's in your "Actor's Business Plan." You decide how often you want to mail and do it until you have a specific reason not to. The key to casting director mailings, which most actors do not fully understand, is that they are most beneficial when done on a regular basis instead of just one time. (The Smart Girls experience with agents is different; they often work with only one mailing.)

Imagine this: You receive a flyer from a small, local unknown Italian restaurant. You're not hungry for Italian food, so you throw away the flyer. A couple weeks later, you're starving for Italian food. You might remember that new restaurant flyer, but it's unlikely, so you probably just go to your usual Italian restaurant. Soon you receive a second flyer from the new Italian restaurant, and this time you keep it. Then next time you want Italian food, you decide to try it out. If you keep getting their flyers, there's a much better chance that you will eventually try them. They are simply reminding people to use their product. You must think of yourself as a "product" and remind the casting executives to call you.

So what kind of mailing plan should you have?
Step One: Identify what areas you want to work in. At Smart Girls, we identify casting directors by the categories of projects they cast: feature films, television series, commercials, or soaps.

Step Two: *Compile your target list. Once you know the areas you* want to work in, then you need to start compiling a list. A good affordable list for most actors would be between 25 to 150 names, mailing to as many as possible based on your budget. Some of my clients mail to as many as 200 to 300 or more on a monthly basis, and you can be sure they are getting calls. You want to include anyone you may have met or auditioned for and anyone who may have seen your work, even if you happened to have made a bad impression (in which case you'll try for a chance to redeem yourself). Once you've identified the people that have been exposed to your incredible talent, then you want to identify those others for whom you would like to read.

Let's say you want to send out to all the current television sitcoms. You can get the Hollywood Reporter or Variety's weekly television production chart for current information. If you go through Smart Girls or if you have a computer, you can keep a running list of your contacts, making it easy to re-contact them each time. Whatever resource you use for addresses, make sure it's updated every 2 to 4 weeks minimally.

Step Three: Determine your marketing budget. What should you allow for marketing in your career? You need to determine what is the most you can spend on marketing your career in light of classes, photos, equipment, books, blood, sweat, tears, desire, time, and belief in yourself. When determining your marketing budget, the costs you have to account for are: headshots, resumes, postcards, personalized message stickers (for the back of your postcard), letters, envelopes (unless you're sending a postcard), current address labels, postage, and the time to put the mailings together. If you're on a tight budget, a good mailing goal to shoot for is 100 casting directors per month.

So now you've compiled your list and you are working on your budget. To keep in touch with industry execs, you can send a headshot package (picture, resume, professional letter), a personalized message postcard, a flyer or postcard about a project you're in, or even a whole newsletter. Nancy Cartwright, the voice of Bart Simpson, sends me, and almost 10,000 other people, The Nancy News every so often with all kinds of news about what's going on with her. Even though people know who she is, the newsletter is great because it reminds her mailing list people that she's available, she's hot, and what's going on in her career.

So what should you send? If you are in a play, you can have flyers or postcards made for it and send those out with a letter, headshot, and resume. But if you're not in a play, you can still write a letter or send a postcard message. In the thousands of letters and postcard messages that I've written, there seems to be a hierarchy of what's most important to highlight to a casting director. It goes something like this:

A) A great agent (if you have a not-so-great agent, don't make a real big deal of it though you can keep their name as the contact).
B) Current or recent high-profile on-camera projects.
C) Current not-so-high-profile on-camera projects in which you have major roles.

D) Past high-profile on-camera projects or projects with top directors or stars.

E) Current small on-camera projects in which you have a small role. Other assets to consider and which fit into the picture based on your age and on-camera credits are theatre experience, training with top coaches or schools, expert level special skills (martial arts), awards and recognition, castability, and personality. All of these pieces should be balanced according to what areas your greatest strengths are.

When composing your letter, write things that show your credibility as an actor and get to the point. Don't ramble on about how you know if you were given a chance, you would be great. When actors come in to work with me, I ask them what sets them apart besides look, talent, commitment, and determination (very common answers from actors). You can also express your personality by adding a humorous tag phrase while stating facts —and yes, that does take some writing ability. I will sometimes describe the actor's persona as such: "Personally, I am __and __" filling in the blanks with appropriate adjectives. Or I'll pitch them in a way that suggests their type: "I've been described as a cross between Jennifer Lopez and Meg Ryan." (Be sure the description is dead-on right and not just wishful thinking or you lose all credibility.) Make your letter or note succinct and informational with style, and whenever possible, personalize it to the individual casting director. Write the most important things first, next most important second, and so forth. I also use bold, caps, italics, and underlining selectively to draw attention to what is most important throughout. As you may gather, writing the letters and messages is a bit of an art form and guessing game. After lots of practice, you'll start to get a sense of what flows and what is important.

How do you know if it's working or when you should try something else? If you're not getting calls, the areas to review are your photo, resume, union affiliations, and agent. If you feel good about the status of those or cannot do anything to improve them for some reason, then look to the messages you're writing in your mailings to see if there's anything you might do more effectively. The bottom line is that everything you do to market yourself is basically done on the faith that it will come through at some point. How long do you give them if they aren't requesting more photos? How many photos will you give your

CHAPTER 7

agent without getting calls before you decide you need new photos or a new agent with more clout? How many auditions do you expect to get from every 100 photos your agent submits? There are no simple, easy, correct answers to these questions. Keep track of these and any statistics to help you make decisions about what's right for you. You simply need to do as many things as you can to market yourself.

Melody Jackson and Smart Girls have currently worked with over 3000 clients. For more information, contact Smart Girls Productions at (323) 850-5778.

MASTER THE ART OF COLD READING

CHAPTER EIGHT

ROUNDING OUT YOUR CAREER
...with other helpful industry services!

Actor's Mailing Services
Follow Up...Follow Up...Follow Up...Follow Up!
Attending cold reading workshops is a valuable tool for an actor's career. But building a successful career takes more than simply attending, no matter how talented you are. One skill that most actors lack is the "follow up". Actors lose out on countless opportunities simply because they fail to follow up.

Casting directors see thousands of actors. Yet actors leave it up to the CDs to follow up. They assume that CDs will do the work to get in contact with them. Or they become intimidated. Many of the CDs bemoan actors mailing or calling or dropping by, or they get hung up on protocol. "Do I send a follow up thank you the day after the workshop?" "Do I send it the following week? "Do I send it the following month?"

By the time most actors get around to following up, they're not sure they even should because so much time has passed. Besides, what do you say? Do you send a headshot or a postcard? Do you wait until your new headshots arrive? Once you've made your decisions, the CD has, indeed, forgotten who you are.

Actor's Mailing Services offers actors a way to follow up...without the hassle. AMS offers a selection of services so that CDs learn who you are and remember who you are. We do the business of the business, so you can concentrate on the art you love.

For more information, contact: Actor's Mailing Services 2118 Wilshire Blvd. PMB 567 Santa Monica, CA 90403. (310) 840-2282. E-mail: actormail@yahoo.com or www.actormail.bigstep.com.

MASTER THE ART OF COLD READING

The Artist's Way Workshop With Kelly Morgan
For Actors and Other Artists

Get out of your own way and make a greater impact. Recover your creativity from blocks including limiting beliefs, fear, self-sabotage, jealousy, guilt.

Recently, in an interview with Susan Sarandon on the Actor's Studio, she said about acting "All it is, is the process. You have to get what you want out of it in the moment you're doing it." ACTING (or a good cold reading) IS AS EASY AND AS DIFFICULT AS STAYING IN THE MOMENT."

The Artist's Way helps an actor stay in the moment by making them a fly on the wall of their own creative process. By simply observing your process, you become more aware of what stops you: the limitations, fears, self-sabotage, jealousy and guilt. With more self-knowledge you make better informed choices about how a character should be interpreted become possible. You won't be unconsciously stuck in your 'stuff'. You'll be more in the moment which increases your impact on those you're reading for.

The Artist's Way Workshop is based on the best-selling book by Julia Cameron who said of the facilitator Kelly Morgan, "You could not find a more sure-footed or inspiring guide. To register for the next 12 week program, call (310) 839-3424.

Casting2000.Com

Preparation is the key to success. Of course, one cannot prepare a cold reading, however, one can be prepared to give an impressive reading in a moment's notice. How? Cold reading workshops!

Delivering an outstanding cold reading is an essential element of what it means to be an actor. The most effective and efficient way to learn the art of cold reading is through cold reading workshops. Workshops provide the actor with the skill, technique, and tempo necessary, allowing you to walk into a cold reading with the grace, serenity, confidence and dignity. Mastering the art of cold reading is an essential part of moving forward in your acting career. It will also give you peace of mind knowing that you can walk into an audition and know matter what they throw at you, you can perform and nail the part.

CHAPTER 8

Another essential element of the profession is "self-promotion". Although it is critical to have a good agent who believes in you, your talent, and your work ethic, it is equally important in the new millennium, to master the art of self-promotion.

The internet has broadened the scope considerably in this area as it has given greater access to actors across the country and around the globe. Your competition is no longer limited to the multitude of actors in your city, state, or country. Casting2000.com has created a unique, cutting edge advantage for you to be seen by some of the industries top agents, managers, and casting directors. Casting2000.com is a user-friendly web site that offers casting directors access to talent twenty-four hours a day, seven days a week. They can view your headshot and resume online, which is also printable on a single sheet of paper for their convenience. Other features include the option to view a demo audio or video reel as well as e-mail directly to you, the talent they seek!

If you are serious about the commitment you have made to your acting career, then you must always be a step ahead of the pack. Check out our web site at www.Casting2000.com or e-mail us at castme@Casting2000.com for details on how to take your career to new heights in the new millennium.

Castnet
Since the official launch of our first application, Castnet.com, in October, 1996, thousands of actors have been searched and submitted electronically by casting directors and talent agents across the United States. Castnet.com is currently used by over 32,000 working actors, 300 casting directors and 185 guild-franchised talent agencies. Every single item on your resume is searchable by casting directors. In addition to being electronically submittable by your agent(s), members of Castnet are entitled to a whole range of member services, such as free sides, resume updates, postcards you can print out or email to 240+ casting directors, free mailing labels, a professional actors forum, portfolio submissions to SAG franchised agents, as well as maps & directions. Castnet's service also allows casting directors to access actor's videos and audio tapes at the click of a mouse. Castnet uses its own private network which does not rely on the internet. This allows for superior reliablility, speed and performance.

All of these services, when fully used, are designed to save you much more than the cost of your Castnet membership.

For more information or to join Castnet, call 1888-873-7373 or check out our website at Castnet.com.

Empowerment For Actors
Christina Kokubo

Empowerment For Actors is a powerful one-on-one exercise which quickly connects the actor into the script through an organic, emotionalized and highly energized inner life. The exercise is cumulative, like working out in the gym. When the actor gains strength, he/she is able to channel more energy and emotional power. In a cold reading, without the benefit of rehearsal and research, the actor must quickly go within to find the life which connects him/her into the script. The only way to achieve a successful cold reading, is to bring an emotional life which is so full, the actor literally trembles with a radiance and vitality which breathes a reality into the script. The actor will believe he or she is living in the truth of the character which causes the audience to be transported with the performance. This takes "the actor's muscle." No matter how free an actor is, it is rare to see a cold reading where the actor becomes the character and produces a mesmerizing performance. Empowerment For Actors is an inner tune-up which can bring the actor to a level where he/she transforms the script into a moment in time where the world stands still and audience breathes as one with the character.

Empowerment For Actors is a conditioning exercise, not an acting class. The work has been developed from Warren Robertson's exercise technique, Alexander Lowen and Wilheim Reich. It is a highly individual process as each actor has a unique history, rhythm, energy and musicality. It is a one-on-one process given with meticulous personal attention, in small groups of four or five actors per session. A free introductory session is offered. For further information: (323) 660-4607 or Metnitiger@earthlink.net.

CHAPTER 8

In The Moment
Robyn Corulla Lee

In The Moment looks at that space between you and the world. It illuminates and helps you stand on the bedrock of your self and your art. The rigors and stresses of trying to be creative at the professional level undermine the very impulses and instincts we need. Each of us has to devise a process to reach our true and serene selves. Many techniques cater to this problem of "making us real" but In The Moment invites the defensive, frightened, and even paralyzed, performer to a true, neutral, and objective state, which allows him to spontaneously go in any direction, and keeps him alive to his own inspiration. In The Moment deals with what is underneath "technique".

It is this place where feelings, personal wisdom, and untouched inspiration live and can be accessed. Expressing instinct and passion as they are in their pure state requires practice. You can learn to live and perform one moment to the next, without being influenced by your fears, expectations, depression, or other threats. And so our real lifetime task is to reclaim our natural gifts. This is the work of In The Moment.

You can learn to function creatively no matter what the inner or outer pressures. The pursuit of our inner gifts includes stamina and concentration, character and nobility, and a burning need to live your life as if you are living art.

A professional career in the arts has never been more hazardous. The sheer number of people wanting to be actors is daunting. The effort the newcomer must make is huge and the encouragement and rewards are few. This scarcity and negativity are additional blows beyond what life normally offers to the creative spirit, the individual confidence and joi de vivre.

The passionate practice of living In The Moment leads you to inspire others to feel the freedom, the massive movement of energy that lives inside all of us. This brave deep work always leads to insight and brilliance.

For more information, call Ms. Lee at (323) 646-8806 or e-mail her at robynlee@aol.com.

MASTER THE ART OF COLD READING

The Monologue Works
Michael Merton

Some actors feel that cold readings are useless. I disagree. Have you ever driven home from an audition and suddenly flashed on a brilliant way that you could have read the scene? Well, that idea was already in your head, you just needed to access it more quickly than you did. Cold reading forces you to exercise your imagination so that you can jump-start your creative process instantly. The more you do it the easier it gets. Obviously, the more time you have to prepare for a role the better. Preparation is a critical component of acting. Ironically, the more prepared you are the more free and spontaneous you can be.

For those times when you are offered the option of performing your own material, it is important to have a prepared monologue or scene in your arsenal of acting tools. Be sure to have one that allows you to showcase those qualities that make you special, and provides an opportunity to display a flow of emotion. In creating monologues and scenes for actors, I stress to them how important it is for their character to start in one emotional place and end in another. A monotonous audition piece does you a disservice. You have two to three minutes to show a casting director that you have colors - show them more than one.

Mr. Merton, a two time EMMY Award nominee, creates and writes original characters and scenarios for monologues and scenework tailored specifically to each actor. Direction and coaching services are also available. To make an appointment to browse through scene and monologue samples, call 323-469-3293.

Nowcasting.Com Actor Services

NowCasting.com offers a variety of actor services related to networking, marketing and electronic submissions. Services include: Sides Access, Searchable CD Database, CD Guide, CD Labels, Agency Labels, Now Casting Notices, Streaming Demo Reel, Searchable Photographer Database (My8x10.com) and more! Services are available a la carte or in several monthly membership packages.

The online actor portfolio: resume, bio and up to 6 headshots is FREE to the professional actor – the actor who is represented by a franchised agent, established manager and/or is a member of an actor guild/union. As of March 2003, there were over 17,000 actors in the online database. Casting Directors are currently using the electronic submissions system – saving valuable time and money - while posting projects, scheduling auditions and fulfilling all their casting needs with just a click of a mouse.

Agents and Managers can put their entire rosters online, encouraging their clients to complete their profiles. With a complete, up-to-date client profile roster, an agency or manager can easily keep track of client info and immediately submit any client's portfolio via the internet.

NowCasting.com (formerly known as LA Actors Online) is run by actors FOR actors and is dedicated to providing the best marketing and networking tools available to the business-minded actor.

WMA Associates
Doug Eakins
Once you have honed your cold reading skills and participated in casting director showcases, it is imperative that you keep in touch with these casting directors. You need to market yourself and make sure your headshots are continually reaching the casting directors' desks.

WMA Associates will aid you by getting your headshots to the right casting directors and having your pictures submitted to the right projects. Over 90% of WMA's clients get auditions or jobs!

WMA Associates submits your headshots to a wide range of projects and casting directors. The following is a partial list of the type of projects you may choose to have your headshots submitted to: films in development, films in preparation, films in pre-production, union films, non-union films, theatrical and commercial casting directors, AFTRA projects, soap operas, theatre productions, graduate and student films. You will also receive a detailed list of every project and casting director where your headshots have been submitted.

For more details and pricing information, contact WMA Associates at (818) 708-0242.

CHAPTER NINE
IF YOU'RE ONLINE...

The following sites have been found helpful to the entertainment industry, especially actors.

www.acadpd.org - Academy Players Directory
www.actorsite.com - Actorsite - Resource Site for Actors
alt.acting - USENET Newsgroup for Actors
www.breakdownservices.com - Actors Access - Breakdowns for Actors
www.castnet.com - Online Actor/Casting Service
www.castingworkbook.com - Online Actor/Casting Service
www.castingworkbook.com/btn – Online African American Casting Service
www.castingworkbook.com/latinheat – Online Latino Casting Service
entertainmentemployers.com - Employment Service Directory
epguides.com - Episodic Guide
www.filmscouts.com - Reviews of Movies, including film festivals
hcdonline.com - Hollywood Creative Directory
www.imdb.com - Internet Movie Database
www.ibdb.com - Internet Broadway Database
www.mapquest.com - Mapquest - Driving Directions and Maps
www.playbill.com - Playbill - Worldwide Theatre Information
script-o-rama.com - Television and Movie Scripts
www.showfax.com - Showfax Sides for Actors
www.wolfesden.net - Chat Board for Professional Actors

UNIONS
www.actra.com
www.aftra.com
www.dga.com
www.sag.com
www.wga.com

PUBLICATIONS
www.backstagewest.com
www.hollyvision.com
www.hollywoodreporter.com
www.reelwest.com
www.blacktalentnews.com
www.variety.com
www.theatrebayarea.com

MASTER THE ART OF COLD READING

INDUSTRY ASSOCIATIONS
www.emmys.org - Academy of Television Arts and Sciences
www.oscars.org - Academy of Motion Picture Arts and Sciences

APPENDICES

The following forms are included to help you make the most of your cold reading workshop experience. Take notes, ask questions, keep a journal of who you met and whatever you think will be helpful for you when you're called in to audition for them. The following pages are useful examples in keeping accurate records. Copy and utilize these or come up with a plan that works for you.

Sample Questions to Ask in a Workshop

When you're in a cold reading workshop, be sure to ask good questions that will help better acquaint you with the industry guest as well as the BUSINESS of the industry. Each guest has individual styles and views. Listen to the other questions being asked as well. There may be something you hadn't thought of or were also interested in. The following are samples to help you get ahead.

1. What do you expect from an actor when they see you at your office?
2. How often do you like to receive post cards?
3. Do you see theatre?
4. Do you review reels?
5. Do you readers for auditions?
6. If an actor gets off to a bad start in their audition, should they ask to start again?
7. How do you feel about actors not sticking to the words in the script?
8. What are your pet peeves? Preferences?
9. Do you call in an actor regardless if they have representation?
10. How do you feel about props/miming/dress at an audition?
11. Do you cast from the internet?

SAMPLE FOLLOW-UP POST CARD

Dear (GUEST NAME),

I had a great time reading for you at the cold reading workshop at (WORKSHOP NAME AND LOCATION) on (DATE). Thank you for sharing your comments and your insight on the entertainment industry. I look forward to the opportunity to audition for you in the near future.

Warmest regards,

NOTE: Sending a follow-up note or post card is strongly recommended. It is good manners and good business. You may also use the post card to let them know what you can be seen in and where. Let them know you're busy!

SAMPLE INFORMATION FORM

Date: 11/17/02
Workshop Attended: Be A Star
Guest: Sandra Wilson
Phone: (310) 555-1234
Assistant: Kathy Smith
Fax/Email: (310) 555-1235
Address: 0000 S. Ventura Blvd. Sherman Oaks 90000
Permanent Address: 0000 N. Pico Blvd.   Los Angeles 90000
Associate(s): Tim White & Sharon Jones
Past Projects: MOW - "Last Dying Days"
                 TV Sitcom - "Happy Years"

Current Projects: Feature Film - "Today's Mobsters"

Future Projects: Casting now for dramatic series - "I'll See You in Court"

Pre-casting Career: Elementary School Teacher
Married X   Single   Divorced   Children 3
Birthday: 12/25
College attended: USC   Originally from: Dayton, OH
Uses workshop actors: Yes   X   No
Pet peeves: Showing up late for auditions.
Physical description: Short - redhead - dresses casually - nice smile

SAMPLE INFORMATION FORM

Scene title: SOME LIKE IT HOT

Comments: Scene started out a little shaky. Partner & I communicated well
as the scene progressed. I stumbled over lines. Need better eye contact.

Cold reading suggestions: Guest would like to see me not rely on memory.
Learn to read from the script without appearing awkward.

Follow-up suggestions: Practice reading script & looking natural.

Postcards: Once a month   X   Once a quarter   Twice a year   Never
Attends Plays: Yes   No X
Feedback on cold readings: Agents should call   No calls   X
Auditions: Taped   X   Not taped
Audition information: Come 15 min. early to auditions. Be prepared for script changes. Do not dress exactly like the character.

ABOUT THE AUTHOR

In addition to being head of Heaven Sent Publishing, Angel is the Executive Producer of Heaven Sent Productions. As a producer, she is the recipient of an Outstanding Achievement award from the American Women In Radio and Television for producing the documentary, Due Process of the Law. Angel's documentary about the first African American cartoonist, Morrie Turner, Keeping The Faith With Morrie, holds honors for Best Direction and Best Documentary from the Hollywood Black Film Festival. She is currently working on the 60-minute to be distributed to schools and libraries. In addition, Angel is pursuing a production deal to have Mr. Turner's Wee Pals comic strip made into a television series entitled Rainbow Squad.

Angel is the founder of Smile Productions and produced the Comedy Flavors showcase. She enjoys her ethnic mix and sharing the humor of her heritage with an audience. (Her mother was born in Havana, Cuba and raised in Kingston, Jamaica. Her father is from Hookerton, North Carolina.) Her comedic style has been labeled "classy comedy with a cutting edge." She is a winner of America's Funniest People and she has appeared on BET's Comic View and Show Me the Funny.

Angel received two consecutive Achievement In Radio awards for her outstanding work in the voice-over industry. Her versatility ranges from commercials, narrations, ADR work to cartoons as Rugrats and Captain Planet. Weekdays, she can be heard on the Tom Joyner Morning Show as Doctor Cotton and Coral in the zany radio soap It's Your World. Angel is an active member of Women in Animation, the NAACP Cinema Committee, AFTRA and SAG. For Angel's health tips for actors and movie critiques, visit www.behealthylifestyles.com and click on E-Healthy.

Hailing from Harlem, New York, Angel holds a BS in Radio and Television Production from Cornell University. Angel is a born again Christian and attends the Oasis Church in Hollywood where she is active in the drama and dance ministry.

Angel believes: *"Submit to the Lord whatever you do, and your plans will succeed."* Proverbs 6:13

ABOUT THE EDITOR

Hailing from Connecticut, by way of New York, Shirley Jordan has appeared in numerous stage, television productions and commercials on both coasts. Included in her TV credits are Ally McBeal, E.R., Friends, The West Wing, Yes, Dear, The District, Jamie Kennedy Experiment, and The Division. She appeared in the films Fortunate Son (opposite Michael Beach) and as the lead in The Abortion of Mary Williams, both on SHOWTIME. As a voice-over artist, she can be heard as the narrator on the audio CD of Z Z Packer's "Drinking Coffee Elsewhere". Onstage, Shirley has appeared in everything from musicals and live industrials to staged readings, comedies and dramas.

Previously, Shirley was a writer/executive editor for the trade publication, Black Talent News, where she wrote cover stories on stars and newcomers, always with a positive eye towards advice and ideas. Later, as a career consultant, she passed along those ideas to actors beginning a career in the entertainment industry. Soon, opportunities presented themselves for her to use her skills as a director, acting coach, and dialogue coach for many professionals in the industry, which she continues to do today. Shirley's writing abilities have led her to pen various bios, one-acts (with John Ewaniuk), edit novels and work on screenplays.

Cold reading has long been an integral part of Shirley's career. By attending these information packed workshops she has successfully obtained representation, countless auditions and, subsequently, work as an actor. "These workshops do more than pay for themselves in the long run. You just have to be willing to invest in yourself, your career. Sure, anyone can show up at an audition, but without cold reading techniques under your belt, chances are slim that you'll make a good impression. And knowing what you're doing certainly makes the audition process more fun and productive for everyone."

Shirley is married to her very loving and supportive husband, Jeff Shafer. Together they have a beautiful eleven -year old son, Jordan Shafer.

APPENDICES

BE A VOLUNTEER/INTERN FOR HEAVEN SENT PUBLISHING

Learn more about the acting business by doing research, networking and other valuable tasks.

Tasks will be tailored to the person according to their skills.

Fax, e-mail or mail your work resume and/or performing resume with a short note or letter.

Mail:	Angel Harper
	1950 Tamarind Avenue # 115
	Los Angeles, CA 90068

Email:	angelharper@earthlink.net
	www.coldreading.com

As usual, any and all comments, testimonials, additional information are welcome. We would like to keep this book as beneficial and up to date as possible. We appreciate your help and support. Please send all comments to the addresses above.

MASTER THE ART OF COLD READING

BOOK LOCALES AND "SPECIAL ORDER" CONTACTS
Look for Master the Art of Cold Reading at your local theatrical bookstores as well as the following places:

BOOK LOCALES
Samuel French Bookstores
7653 Sunset Blvd
Los Angeles, CA
(323) 876-0570 (Hollywood)
(818) 762-0535 (San Fernando Valley)

Barnes And Noble
barnesandnoble.com
100 Middlesex Blvd
Customer Orders-Facility 2014
Jamesburg, NJ 08831 USA
(723) 656-2000
(723) 274-9703 Chris Weiss

Baker & Taylor Books
Buying Department
P.O. Box 8888
Momence, Il 60954-1799
(815) 472-2444

Borders Books
330 S. La Cienega Blvd.
Los Angeles, CA 90036
(310) 659-4045

SPECIAL ORDERS
Amazon.com
sp.orders@amazon.com
700 5th Avenue, 26th Fl
Seattle, WA 98104
(800) 510-1454 ex 66717

APPENDICES

AP Special Project
Amazon.com
PO Bx 24983
Seattle, WA 98124-0983
(800) 441-8614
(877) 327-2191 fax

BookSurge, LLC
www.booksurge.com
Mitchell Davis, VP Marketing
Newauthor@booksurge.com
(866) 308-6235 ext. 38

ISBN#'s:
5th Ed. 0-9630551-2-7
6th Ed. 0-9630551-4-3

A Very Special Thanks

Thank you for purchasing this copy of Master The Art of Cold Reading. In doing so, you are not only helping yourself to further your career, but you are contributing to a much larger cause as well. A portion of the proceeds from this book will be donated to the Motion Picture & Television Fund.

www.ingramcontent.com/pod-product-compliance
Lightning Source LLC
Chambersburg PA
CBHW070455090426
42735CB00012B/2567